PURGATORY

MICHAEL J. TAYLOR, S.J.

PURGATORY

Our Sunday Visitor Publishing Division
Our Sunday Visitor, Inc.
Huntington, Indiana 46750

ISBN: 0-87973-955-X
LCCCN: 98-65359

Cover design by Tyler Ottinger
Printed in the United States of America
955

⁓ Contents ⁓

Chapter 1
State of the Question 7

Chapter 2
Genesis of a Doctrine 17

Chapter 3
Is Purgatory Still a Reasonable Belief? 39

Chapter 4
Reflections on Common Objections to Purgatory 55

Chapter 5
Thoughts on the "Final Option" 69

Chapter 6
Death: A Speculative Scenario 75

Chapter 7
Praying for the Dead 83

Appendix
The Graphic Imagery of Purgatory 89

Epilogue 103

Glossary 104

Select Bibliography 106

Scriptural Index 109

Index of Names and Subjects 110

Chapter 1

• ͜ •

State
of the Question

Is the concept of purgatory disappearing from Catholic belief and consciousness? Older believers hold vivid memories of the "place" — a temporary post-death state where penitent Christians are purified from the effects of their sins. This must happen, it is thought, because believers should be fully cleansed of their selfishness before they enter heaven. As the Book of Revelation says of heaven, "nothing unclean will enter it" (Rv 21:27).

A growing number of the faithful, however, seem to have only the vaguest ideas about purgatory. If they show interest in the idea at all it is marginal. In earlier times Catholics remembered the spiritual needs of their departed relatives and friends through their prayers and good works, and especially by remembering them at Mass. Now the accepted premise seems to be that all who die as believers "live with the Lord." In death they have reached paradise. Rather than three possibilities for the dead, many see only two, heaven or hell, with heaven quickly claiming all but the totally evil. It would be a stretch to refer to any deceased Christians as "poor souls." Even theologians who address the subject of death seem reluctant to speak about any possible need for further purification of the dead before they gain access to the vision of God.

And yet purgatory remains an "official and defined teaching" of the Church and has been so since the Second Council of Lyons (1274). Its doctrinal status was reconfirmed at the councils of Florence (1439) and Trent (1563). These councils speak of a post-death process of purification where sinners more fully atone and satisfy for their offenses against God and neighbor. In this purifying work these councils taught the dead can be assisted by the prayers, good works, and offered Masses of the living. This is so because Christians believe firmly in a vital spiritual communion of love and support between the living and the dead for the spiritual welfare of both. The gospel teaches that all Christians are members of the one Christ:

> As a body is one though it has many parts, and all the parts of the body, though many, are one body, so also Christ. In one Spirit we were all baptized into one body, whether Jews or Greeks, slaves or free persons, and we were all given to drink of one Spirit. Now the body is not a single part, but many (1 Cor 12:12-14).

Why Less Interest in Purgatory?

Why has the concept of purgatory lost credibility with so many Catholics? Why have they dismissed a traditional belief as a forgettable relic of their medieval past? One can cite several reasons for this.

First, we note new attitudes and approaches to death and

funerals have occurred among the faithful because of recent changes in Church practice. Since the rites for funerals underwent reform with the Second Vatican Council, the new liturgy has resulted in bringing about a change in the way Catholics view death and the afterlife. Where earlier the stress at funerals was on the deliverance of the deceased from remaining harmful effects of their sins (even rescue from the "gates of hell"), the emphasis has turned to focus almost exclusively on the unity of the Christian with Christ and his Resurrection.

An example of this new liturgical emphasis can be seen in an optional prayer often used in the opening rites for funerals:

> Welcome, O Lord, the departed into the company of your saints, into your heavenly kingdom of light and peace. As Christ was raised from death, we pray that our brother/sister, baptized in his name, be united with his Resurrection and clothed with his glory. Almighty Father, source of all life, grant N., full union with your Spirit. May death be for him/her a homecoming into your presence.

Surely the Risen Christ grants forgiveness to all who believe in him. If forgiven, why should there be concern about the effects of one's sins? Jesus' merciful pardon would seem powerful enough to remove these as well. Even the somber "black" of the Requiem Mass, with its connotation of sinful unworthiness, has given way to the more joyful and reassuring "white" of the Resurrection.

This new emphasis has worked subtle changes in Christian attitudes toward belief in purgatory. As one concentrates on one's unity with Jesus' Resurrection and God's unquestionable desire to forgive the offenses of believers, thoughts naturally turn toward the nearness of departed Christians to heaven. If forgiven, why should there be delay in reaching it? In earlier times Christians seemed more conscious of their sinfulness, their many weaknesses. Most felt unworthy to see and be with God so quickly. Instinctively they felt a need for more intense spiritual purification before heavenly intimacy with God could take place. Now death seemed like sure access to God and paradise. The Requiem Mass with its somber ambience made the point that, though death brought the departed closer to God, it also meant they likely faced further purification before they experienced a full sharing in his glory. No one doubted that faithful Christians would ultimately reach God, but the older rite implied that further work could well be in the picture before that blessed day.

The new rite with its aura of joy and sense of "heavenly arrival" seems to rule out any need for survivors to help the dead reach their eternal fulfillment. Funeral sermons and other testimonies are mostly celebratory eulogies containing memorable highlights of a person's life. Rarely is mention ever made of regrettable imperfections or spiritual incompleteness in the personal history of the departed. Few urge mourners to remember the dead in their prayers by asking that God mercifully and quickly grant them eternal peace. Celebration implies one's life is essentially complete with death. Little more need be done except to say our temporary good-byes.

But the demands of the gospel imply that more is necessary than the simple living out of a life, however interesting. It asks believers to live their lives properly, and in their reflective and introspective moments most Christians would admit they often fall short of this ideal. Much of what God asked them to do they have not done. In a way they die "incomplete," their life's work unfinished. But today any thought of further work yet to be done in purgatory is lost in the assumption that the believer at death dwells with God almost immediately.

Though older Christians continue to remember their dead at Mass, to offer spiritual assistance to them through their prayers and good works, younger believers seem content to treasure good thoughts and memories about the departed and leave it at that. They see no need to offer them spiritual help of any sort. If death equals immediate access to glory, why should they worry about the sins of their friends, or God's judgment on their lives?

Beyond the new celebratory approach to death and funerals, another liturgical change has had subtle effects on people's belief in purgatory — the sacrament of anointing (earlier called the "last rites" or "Extreme Unction"; now more often described as the "Sacrament of the Sick"). Since this sacrament formerly was given only to the seriously ill, it elicited a feeling of closeness to death; it was, in fact, often viewed as a preparation for that important milestone. The minister of the anointing spoke of the possible nearness of death and judgment and assured receivers of the sacrament that the prayers and good works of the Church were with them as they faced these critical moments. Today the rite for anointing of the sick and suffering prays predominantly for their recovery.

Free him/her from all harm.

Relieve the sufferings of all the sick.

Give life and health to our brother/sister.

God of mercy, ease the sufferings and comfort the weakness of your servant whom the Church anoints with this holy oil.

May the Lord who frees you from sin save you and raise you up.

For one obviously dying, a prayer is said that God release the person from possible punishments in the life to come, but in the general anointing of the sick there is no mention of possible trials to come. Again, if death is seen as entrance to glory, the anointing must concern itself mainly with the here and now problems of illness.

As Christians more and more stress God's limitless love and readiness to forgive, the idea of sin and judgment becomes less fearsome. If one dies repentant and forgiven, many assume the effects of sin are taken away also. God's boundless love would seem to erase our unworthiness and render us capable of receiving his love fully. A purificational delay after death seems unwarranted.

It should be noted also that in the past twenty years or so we have seen remarkable changes in the way people view the idea of sin. In former times, sin was seen as an act that offended God. It was the breaking of his laws. It deserved punishment and demanded restitution and repair. Serious sin severed one's union with God. He alone could reunite and reconcile the sinner with himself. And so his absolution and reconciliation must be sought to undo it.

Today sin is often spoken of as the disruption or injuring of a relationship. Sin compromises the love, unity and harmony that should exist between God and his creatures. When we sin, our lives go off-track somewhat. Christ must come to restore good relations between us and God. He must redirect our lives and put them on the rightful path to God. From our earlier biblical traditions we saw our sins as having evil consequences that called for punishment, expiation, reparation. This new understanding has made Christians more concerned about the overall direction of their lives. They seem less worried about the seriousness of their individual here-and-now sins and their reparation, a fact made manifest by the infrequency of the use of the Sacrament of Penance and Reconciliation. If sin is less a cause for serious concern now, in the thinking of many contemporary believers, it can only be less worrisome for life beyond death. And as people today seem less bothered by the temporal repercussions of their sins, this removes another reason for belief in a process designed to overcome these effects in the life to come.

We also note that in recent years there has emerged a new theology of death. Traditionally death marked the definitive end of one's earthly life. It was the time when God would pass judgment on how one lived it. The decisions, choices, and direction of a lifetime had been made or chosen. One's life was over and the person stood passive before God. He alone was active in the determination of the eternal fate of the dead. Now some theologians see death not simply as an act that happens to an individual, a passive event. It is an act of the dying person in which he or she makes a final choice for or against God. In a sense death does not set in motion God's judgment of us. More properly it presents the opportunity for us to make a lasting personal decision for or against him. That choice determines our eternal destiny. This final option would not be made before or after death. It would be made in the moment of death.

In this "moment" all the dying will have full consciousness and complete freedom. Their powers of decision-making will be totally clear and will be made with full awareness of all their important life choices up to that point. What may have been vague and uncertain choices in life will now be firmly made; the best of former options will be ratified in a final way. Our eternity, these theologians insist, must not be based on vague, ambivalent, uncertain options and commitments, but only on the clearest, freest and most authentically made personal decision. As dying persons face this option for God, they will see where in God's plan they should have fitted in, not only in their individual human histories, but also in God's cosmic scheme of creation. In death the dying must opt either to embrace God's plan, their proper place in his cosmos, or to reject it. An eternity with God or without him, a life of self-love or one of outward-directed self-lessness, depends on this final option. In a way God does not put people in heaven or hell. They do this themselves by the option they make in death. Though these theologians see people's historical choices orienting them toward the option they will make at death, it is mainly that *final one* that determines their eternity.

This new theory as generally put forth has no traditional precedent in Christian history, but it seems philosophically based on God's will to save *all* of his creatures, as expressed, for example, in 1 Timothy 2:3-6:

> God our savior . . . wills everyone to be saved
> and to come to knowledge of the truth. For there
> is one God. There is also one mediator between
> God and the human race, Christ Jesus, himself
> human, who gave himself as ransom for *all*.

This text points out the universal salvific will of God. To these theologians it implies that he will give all, even agnostics and rejecters, the chance of a saving choice. His love and mercy demand this. Since such paramount emphasis is given to this final option, these people give only slight consideration to any sort of purgatory that might be consequent to the making of this option. Again, such a theology of death contributes to the decline of serious concern about an extended temporary state of purification for the dead.

And, of course, it goes without saying that the temper of our secularized times gives scant attention to life's deeper meaning and purpose. For all too many what seems to count is the present and immediate future, with its desires for pleasure, self-satisfaction and "personal fulfillment." Life after death seems questionable at best. If anything, death is seen as an ending, not as a possible new beginning following judgment. Catholics living in such a society can hardly be unaffected by its materialistic indifference to spiritual values. And sadly we must admit that although many instructional and study programs are available, the spiritual education of Catholics, young and old, seems much less in evidence today than in the past. The times obviously call Catholics to devote more energy and seriousness to their spiritual education and development.

So it appears that several recent changes in Church practice, along with new theological developments, are to a degree responsible for the current minimal interest in the concept of purgatory. The new celebratory funeral rites with their emphasis on the proximity of the dead to resurrection and eternal joy contrast sharply with the largely petitionary cast of earlier rites of Requiem, where prayers were said for the dead to deliver them from the spiritually harmful effects of their sins and shortcomings. There has been a *de facto* transformation of the Sacrament of Extreme Unction (last rites) from a sacrament of preparation for death and judgment into a sacrament mainly of healing. Theologians engage in new thinking about sin, where it is seen less as an offense against God's law requiring reparation and expiation, and more as the injuring of a relationship that needs correction and revitalization. We also note the recent theoretical efforts at fashioning a new theology of death where critical importance is given to the concept of a final option for or against God at the moment of death, which has a determining effect on one's eternal destiny. Finally, the mood and temper of our self-absorbed, secularistic times make discussion of life's final and deeper purposes difficult to command people's notice.

All these changes and developments have worked to draw people's attention and interest away from purgatory as a believable part of God's plan to save the world. Today, though the doctrine remains solidly in the psychic subconscious of many Catholics, intelligent discussion and reflection on the subject of purgatory as a state awaiting many Christians is largely missing from the contemporary theological scene.

Notwithstanding, many still retain strong belief in the existence and need for a "place" or "state" like purgatory. Before we make a case for its existence, it may be helpful to review briefly some of the historical highlights that led to the development and definition of this belief. With a general recall of purgatory's origins and the rationale given for it, we will be in a better position to recommend a more compelling interpretation of the doctrine, one that could perhaps have more meaning for contemporary Catholics.

Chapter 2

* ⁀ *

Genesis
of a Doctrine

Though belief in the general concept of a "place" like purgatory can be traced back to the third century, the Church did not give it the status of official teaching until the Second Council of Lyons in the thirteenth century (1274). This council was concerned about restoring unity between the Eastern and Western Churches; part of the discussions attempted to reconcile the beliefs of the two Churches with respect to the status of the dead, especially the lot of repentant sinners. This reunification effort continued at the Council of Florence (1438-1439); and again the subject of a post-death process of purification for sinners came up in the discussions. Although efforts to reunify the two Churches failed, the councils did result in defining purgatory as an official teaching of the Catholic Church. Purgatory was further defined by the Church at the Council of Trent (1563).

The Church's teaching on purgatory is briskly summarized in these paragraphs from the *Catechism of the Catholic Church:*

> All who die in God's grace and friendship, but still imperfectly purified, are indeed assured of their eternal salvation; but after death they undergo purification, so as to achieve the holiness necessary to enter the joys of heaven (1030).

> The Church gives the name *Purgatory* to this final purification of the elect, which is entirely different from the punishment of the damned (See Council of Florence (1439): DS 1304; Council of Trent (1563): DS 1820; see also Benedict XII, Benedictus Deus (1336): DS 1000). The Church formulated her doctrine of faith on Purgatory especially at the Councils of Florence and Trent. The tradition of the Church, by reference to certain texts of Scripture, speaks of a cleansing fire (see 1 Cor 3:15; 1 Pet 1:7):

> > "As for certain lesser faults, we must believe that, before the Final Judgment, there is a purifying fire. He who is truth says that whoever utters blasphemy against the Holy Spirit will be pardoned neither in this age nor in the age to come. From this sentence we understand that certain offenses can be forgiven in this age, but certain others in the age to come" (St. Gregory the Great, Dial. 4, 39: PL 77, 396; see Mt 12:31-32) (1031).

This teaching is also based on the practice of

prayer for the dead, already mentioned in Sacred Scripture: "Therefore [Judas Maccabeus] made atonement for the dead, that they might be delivered from their sin" (2 Macc 12:45). From the beginning the Church has honored the memory of the dead and offered prayers in suffrage for them, above all the Eucharistic sacrifice, so that, thus purified, they may attain the beatific vision of God (see Council of Lyons II,1274, DS 856). The Church also commends almsgiving, indulgences, and works of penance undertaken on behalf of the dead (1032).

What these councils said about purgatory was not elaborate in detail. They simply declared that purgatory existed as a "state" (or process). There the "punishments" due sin which had not been satisfied before death were satisfied fully. In purgatory believers were spiritually cleansed and prepared for the eternal vision of God. In the process of purifying the dead from the residues of sin, the prayers and good works of living believers were said to be of great value. In short, the doctrine of purgatory has three components: 1) that a purification after death exists; 2) that it involves some kind of pain; and 3) that the purification of the dead can be assisted by the prayers and offerings of the living. Nothing specific has been taught about the nature, the place or the duration of this purifying process.

What led the Church at these councils to express her belief in purgatory this way? Christians believe that Jesus — through his life, death and Resurrection — has made available to them God's forgiveness. In Christ the world finds full access to his eternal love. Thus believers see an afterlife as a certainty. To reach and realize God's eternal love in this afterlife, Jesus asks that his disciples remain faithful to him and his message. Heaven is reached by living lives of faith, hope and love until they die. Though their lives may be marked by count-less lapses, infidelities, and acts of selfishness, they know if they repent and return to Jesus and re-embrace him and his message, he will forgive them.

They also realize their sins have repercussions that must be removed to assure a true relationship of love to exist be-tween them and God. We have only to recall the opening story of the Bible. Adam sinned by disobeying God. God's reaction to this sin was not indifference or unconcern. He punished Adam severely (Gn 3:17-19). Sin not only brought about estrangement between him and God. The act deserved punishment and created in Adam a need to "pay a price" for his sin. Later in Genesis we find the story of Noah. There God reacted to the sins of the people by destroying them in the flood (Gn 6-9). Again, sin is seen to have effects that call for punishment.

Later still we find God forgiving the doubting Moses, but also depriving him admittance to the promised land (Nm 20:12). David, too, is forgiven his sin of adultery, but suffers the death of the child who resulted from it (2 Sm 12:13-14).

The lesson of these stories is clear — sin displeases God and sinners must suffer punishment and "pay a price" for committing it. Countless times Scripture teaches the lesson that sin is evil. Even so, it can be forgiven, but sin has effects on the sinner and those sinned against. For full res-toration to spiritual health, sinners must address and over-come these effects. If they seem to neglect or escape the consequences of their sins, others somehow must assume the task of doing this. The need for this is at the heart of the gospel:

> Yet it was *our* infirmities that he bore,
> *our* sufferings that he endured,
> While we thought of him as stricken,
> as one smitten by God and afflicted.

But he was pierced for *our* offenses,
crushed for *our* sins,
Upon him was the chastisement that makes us
whole,
by his stripes *we were healed* (Is 53:4-5).

There is also one mediator between God and the
human race, Christ Jesus, himself human, who
gave himself as ransom *for all* (1 Tm 2:5-6).

Since these "sin stories" associate purification or atonement of some sort with the full forgiveness of sin, one can find some grounds for belief in a "place" like purgatory. When Christians actually come to believe in purgatory, it will be seen not so much as a "place" for the forgiveness of unforgiven sin, as the process through which sinners work to expiate the effects of their sins which have not yet been fully requited at death. They should go to God not just forgiven; ideally they should go to him cleansed and free from the infections sin has worked on their souls.

The Scriptural Evidence

Does Scripture in a more direct way speak about a post-death place of purification? There are no texts that exclude the possibility that such a place could exist. As belief in purgatory began slowly to emerge in the consciousness of Christians, several texts became associated with the belief. Perhaps the most explicit is 2 Maccabees 12:39-46. It is worth examining this text in some detail:

On the following day, since the task had now
become urgent, Judas and his men went to gather
up the bodies of the slain to bury them with their
kinsmen in their ancestral tombs. But under the
tunic of each of the dead they found amulets sa-

cred to the idols of Jamnia, which the law forbids the Jews to wear. So it was clear to all that this was why these men had been slain. They all therefore praised the ways of the Lord, the just judge who brings to light the things that are hidden. Turning to supplication, they prayed that the sinful deed might be fully blotted out. The noble Judas warned the soldiers to keep themselves free from sin, for they had seen with their own eyes what had happened because of the sin of those who had fallen.

He then took up a collection among all his soldiers, amounting to two thousand silver drachmas, which he sent to Jerusalem to provide for an expiatory sacrifice. In doing this he acted in a very excellent and noble way, inasmuch as he had the resurrection of the dead in view; for if he were not expecting the fallen to rise again, it would have been useless and foolish to pray for them in death. But if he did this with a view to the splendid reward that awaits those who had gone to rest in godliness, it was a holy and pious thought.

Thus he made atonement for the dead that they might be freed from this sin.

Even though these dead warriors were guilty of sins against the Torah, it was concluded that their cause was far from hopeless. Indeed, the living prayed that God would forgive their sins. In fact, they celebrated sin-offerings for them in Jerusalem. In a sense, these prayers were premised on a belief that future resurrection was possible even for the sinful, especially when the living prayed earnestly for their forgiveness. In this scriptural episode one can find elements of what Christians believe about purgatory — that the living, through their prayers, can help the dead overcome their sins; they can help them realize ultimate salvation, which their unrequited sins prevent them from reaching.

Another text that was often quoted in defense of purgatory is Matthew 12:32:

> And whoever speaks a word against the Son of
> Man will be forgiven; but whoever speaks against
> the holy Spirit will not be forgiven, either in this
> age or in the age to come.

Many hold that this text implies damnation for those who reject God in a definitive way, but the possibility of forgiveness "in the life to come" for those whose sins are not totally evil or damning.

Another New Testament text commonly used in support of purgatory is 1 Corinthians 3:10-15:

> According to the grace of God given to me, like
> a wise master builder I laid a foundation, and another is building upon it. But each one must be
> careful how he builds upon it, for no one can lay
> a foundation other than the one that is there,
> namely, Jesus Christ.
>
> If anyone builds on this foundation with gold,
> silver, precious stones, wood, hay, or straw, the
> work of each will come to light, for the Day will
> disclose it. It will be revealed with fire, and the
> fire (itself) will test the quality of each one's work.
> If the work stands that someone built upon the
> foundation, that person will receive a wage. But
> if someone's work is burned up, that one will suffer loss; the person will be saved, but only as it
> were through fire.

This passage speaks of various ways Christians live their

faith, some with quality and depth of commitment, others with much less seriousness. The text says that God will test the faith of all "by fire," and if in the end believers hold fast to Christ "as their foundation," they will be saved, but only as it were "through fire." Whether the fire is real or metaphorical, many saw in the text a reference to a post-death place of purification where God would test people (even the sinful) with a view to their ultimate salvation. Fire is often a cleansing and purifying agent. Perhaps the "testing by fire" could indicate that God seeks not only to forgive the sinful, but also that he wants to *purify* them from the spiritually debilitating effects of their sins.

Another text, 1 Peter 1:6-7, which uses the image of fire, is sometimes used to lend biblical support for the purificational cleansing of sinners after death: ". . . for a little while you may have to suffer through various trials, so that the genuineness of your faith, more precious than gold that is perishable even though tested by fire, may prove to be for praise, glory, and honor at the revelation of Jesus Christ."

The idea that sinners stand in need of God's purifying "fire" derives from Jesus' insistence that heaven is reached only by the selfless and those who strive after holiness. See, for example, such scriptural passages as:

> . . . those who have done good deeds will rise to the resurrection of life, but those who have done wicked deeds will rise to the resurrection of condemnation (Jn 5:29).

> Do you not know that the unjust will not inherit the kingdom of God? (1 Cor 6:9, 10).

> . . . no one will see the Lord without holiness (Heb 12:14).

> . . . But nothing unclean will enter it [the heav-

enly temple], nor any (one) who does abominable things or tells lies. Only those will enter whose names are written in the Lamb's book of life (Rv 21:27).

Many exegetical scholars today doubt that there is clear implication of purgatory in any of these texts. Nevertheless, as Christians gradually developed a belief in a place of purification beyond death, these texts seemed to give them some biblical support. The instinct of Christians was to pray for their dead to forestall possible delays in their reaching God and at least one of these texts spoke of the value of prayer for the dead, especially for those whose sins may not have been adequately atoned for and who stood in need of God's purifying cleansing.

In addition to these texts, the New Testament often taught believers their faith and baptism joined them to each other in a communion of love and prayer. Consider, for example, Paul's words in 1 Corinthians:

> Do you not know that you are the temple of God, and that the Spirit of God dwells in you? If anyone destroys God's temple, God will destroy that person; for the temple of God, which you are, is holy (3:16-17).

> Are you unaware that your bodies are members of Christ? (6:15).

> Because the loaf of bread is one, we, though many, are one body, for we all partake of the one loaf (10:17).

> As a body is one though it has many parts, and all the parts of the body, though many, are one body, so also Christ. For in one Spirit we were all

> baptized into one body, whether Jews or Greeks,
> slaves or free persons, and we were all given to
> drink of one Spirit. Now the body is not a single
> part, but many (12:12-14).

This mystical union did not cease with death. As Christians could help and support one another through their prayers during their earthly lives, they could and should support each other in death.

Still, it must be admitted that specific scriptural evidence for the existence of a place like purgatory is slight. However, when we examine the Church's evolving tradition, the evidence becomes much stronger. We now in a summary way will investigate some of the historical highlights of that developing tradition.

Early Church Tradition

We can find traces of belief in purgatory as far back as the late second and early third century in the writings of Tertullian (+ 225), Clement of Alexandria (+ ca. 215) and Origen (+ ca. 254). Tertullian refers to the practice of Christians praying for the dead as quite common. He himself recommends it, also suggesting that Masses be offered for the dead. Tomb inscriptions are found in the catacombs indicating the dead sought the prayers of the living to help them find peace and refreshment in the afterlife. Tertullian and others speak of visions pious believers had of departed souls seeking their help for release from their sufferings. Though we might wonder whether these visions reflect the actual circumstances of the dead, they seem to articulate a developing consciousness on the part of the faithful that there is a place where some souls are purified after death (presumably from the injurious effects of their sins).

A famous illustration of such visions is Tertullian's account of the acts of the martyrdom of St. Perpetua in which she recounts a dream she had of her dead brother Dinocrates, who died quite young of cancer:

> That very night, this was shown to me in a vision: I saw Dinocrates going out from a gloomy place, where also there were several others, and he was parched and very thirsty, with a filthy countenance and pallid color, and with the wound he had on his face when he died. This Dinocrates had been my brother after the flesh, seven years of age, who died miserably with disease . . . For him I had made my prayer, but between him and me there was a large separation, so that neither of us could approach the other. . . . and [I] knew that my brother was in suffering. But I trusted that my prayer would bring help to his suffering and I prayed . . . day and night, groaning and weeping that he receive relief. Then, on the day on which we remained in fetters, this was shown to me. I saw that the place which I had formerly observed to be in gloom was now bright; and Dinocrates, with a clean body well clad, was finding refreshment. . . . [And] he went away from the water to play joyously, after the manner of children, and I awoke. Then I understood that he was translated from the place of punishment (*The Martyrdom of Perpetua and Felicity* 2:3-4, A.D. 202).

Vision-stories like Perpetua's showed that Christians at this time believed that some of the dead were suffering for their sins and imperfections (undergoing trials of one sort or another). In addition, these stories informed the living that they could and should help the dead in their trials with their prayers and good works.

Clement of Alexandria (+ ca. 215) speculated about sinners who die repentant, but who failed to do reparative penance for all their sins. With 1 Corinthians 3:10-15 in mind, he seems to say that God purifies such sinners in a spiritually cleansing fire after death. This is so because the dead are still one with Christ the "purifier" and "transformer" through their baptism. In death he continues to transform his imperfect disciples to prepare them for resurrection and glory. He also teaches that Christians can bear the burdens of fellow believers, both the living and the dead. They can assist the spiritual needs of other Christians, for they mutually share a spiritual union with them through faith that continues beyond death. And indeed if departed sinners are undergoing a "purifying fire," the inference is that the living by their prayers can assist them spiritually in that process (*Stromata* 3.16, 4.24, 5.14, 7.6, 7.12).

Origen (+ ca. 254), like Clement, also clearly taught that the souls of the dead could be purified by God's "spiritual fire" after death. Though painful, this "fire" was seen to be spiritually maturing more than punitive. It prepared the imperfect dead for ultimate salvation. Origen saw the duration of purification depending on the seriousness of the sins of the departed.

Cyprian of Carthage (+ 258) reasoned that just as the sins of Christians can be forgiven, their effects overcome in this life, so also it is likely they can be purified in the world to come.

It seems, then, in the writings of Tertullian, Clement, Origen and Cyprian we can find the root elements of purgatory. They all variously state that as people are capable of purification now, purification is possible for them also in the next life.

Augustine's view (+ 430) constitutes a major step forward in the developing belief in a post-death place of purification for sinners. In his *Confessions* he speaks about the death of his mother, Monica, who, though a good and admirable woman, was subject to human frailties and imperfections. His love for her was so strong that he instinctively sought to assist her spiritual needs in death with his prayers. In fact, Monica had sought him to do that before she died. Especially she wanted him to remember her at the offering of the Mass, the memorial of Christ's victory over all sin. In his solicitude for his mother's eternal welfare, Augustine finds a wholesome remedy for the grief he feels at her passing.

Augustine finds biblical warrant for his prayers in the words of Paul, 1 Corinthians 3:10-15. To him the text seems to refer not only to God's purification of sins in this life; it refers to their atonement in the next. He believes the living can offer Masses, as well as their alms, good works and prayers to assist the dead in overcoming their sins. He urges that this be done for those who generally lived good lives, but who were sinful at times. Though forgiven, such sinners must still be subject to God's "purgatorial fire" for the remission of the damaging effects of their sins. He assumes God's purification of the dead, though psychically painful, is temporal. Its sufferings are cleansing and redemptive and infallibly lead the departed to glory. In Augustine's writings can be found all the elements that later will be accepted and solidified in the Church's teaching on purgatory. His opinions will be given great weight from his time on.

We find his views summarized in a passage from his *Handbook on Faith, Hope, and Charity*:

> The time which interposes between the death of a man and the final resurrection holds souls in hidden retreats, accordingly as each is deserving of rest or of hardship, in view of what the person merited when living in the flesh. Nor can it be denied that the souls of the dead find relief through the piety of their friends and relatives who are still alive, when the Sacrifice of the Mediator

[Mass] is offered for them, or when alms are given in the Church. But these things are of profit to those who, when they were alive, merited that they might afterward be able to be helped by these things. There is a certain manner of living, neither so good that there is no need of these helps after death, nor yet so wicked that these helps are of no avail then (29:109).

Later Development of the Doctrine

In the Western Church, Augustine's views on post-death purgation continued to dominate theological thought. A purgatory of some sort was seen as necessary for the dead because sinners must cleanse the roots of sin from their souls.

Theologians in the Eastern Church speak of post-death purification also, but they stress the process is more concerned with healing the wounds of sin than atoning for them through suffering. Ever increasing numbers of Christians took for granted that purgation of some kind would be a part of the life of sinners after death. Both Eastern and Western authorities urged the faithful to pray for the dead. Prayer and good works were seen as most helpful in assisting them in the purificational process.

After Augustine, people became more conscious that penance and purification constitute an integral part of the forgiveness of their sins. As they sought to assist the dead in expiating their sins, they were moved to do more penance for the expiation of their own. The emerging idea of something like a purgatory was not the coining of a new doctrine. In many ways it was a corollary of the mystery of forgiveness. Jesus not only wanted sinners to be sorry for their sins; he wanted them responsibly to repair the damages their sins do.

As Christians more and more associated a willingness to do penance and perform good works with genuine sorrow for their sins, they knew many people died having done too little atoning penance. It seemed inevitable, therefore, that they would face this task after death, for no one can share glory unless they are completely cleansed of their sins (see again Jn 5:29, etc., page 24).

Since no one had personal experience of how the needed purificational work took place in the afterlife, Christians let their imaginations conjure up spatial and temporal images for the process, e.g., they had to locate a forbidding "place" for the purifying process; sentences of varying length for specific types of sins had to be determined and described, the more lurid and frightening the better. The point, after all, was to chasten sinners to live more virtuous, less sinful lives and the vivid images motivated them to do the lion's share of their atoning works before death.

Pope Gregory the Great (+ 604) exerted a large influence on the furtherance of belief in a place of purification for the dead. In his writings Gregory instilled in people strong belief in the afterlife. Like earlier authorities, he stressed how valuable the prayers of the living were for the purgatorial needs of the dead and urged the faithful to pray earnestly for departed souls. He made believers more conscious of the damaging effects of their sins. Forgiveness may remove sin from the soul, but it does not take away the residues of selfishness that prompt people to sin. These are progressively removed by acts of selflessness. If people fail to expiate their selfish acts before death, the need to do so remains after death. If one dies in a state of unrequited selfishness, where will the atoning work be done?

Gregory is not always clear on how and where this will be done, but he seems to favor the place where sins were committed as the best location for their expiation. Sinful souls, he assumed, would thus return to earth for this necessary work. His thoughts about sin and the need for departed sinners to purify themselves from its infectious remnants were embodied in highly imaginative stories and legends. These stories were didactic in purpose. The penances that sinners were required to perform in these stories showed great creativity, for they always tried to make them suitable for overcoming particular types of sins.

In the century following Gregory (the early Middle Ages) there were no great theological advances that added much light to the evolving concept of purgatory. But these years did see a lively use of the Christian imagination at work as it attempted to visualize and describe the life to come and the expiational work they believed went on there. There were many bridges and valleys to cross, rivers and pits of fire to traverse, suffering through periods of extreme cold, dangerous trips to be made, exaggerated torments of all sorts attached to various and sundry sins.

No one supplied more graphic imagery to describe the purificational process than the Irish. With their native eschatological outlook on life and very inventive imaginations, the Irish depicted a very tough row for sinners to hoe in the afterlife. Sins needed more than forgiveness; their evil effects had to be atoned for either in this life or the next, and the Irish showed great ingenuity in suggesting penances they thought "suitable" for sinners to suffer for particular kinds of sins. Moreover, the bishops and monks in their preaching and counseling ministry saw the frightful imagery as a helpful deterrent to sin as well as a source for sober thinking about the afterlife and judgment. As the Irish missionaries popularized the use of private confession during their evangelical excursions to the continent, they also did much to convince people they could look forward to reparative sufferings after death if their lives were too sinful. They urged the people to pray fervently for the dead. They stood in great need of the prayers and good works of the living for the atonement of their sins (see the Appendix for a more detailed discussion of the imagery of purgatory).

The grotesque, fearful imagery which became associated with the purification of the dead had the effect of solidifying previously accepted beliefs about death and activity that went on in the afterlife before glory was realized. Though the sufferings of the dead were described as difficult and demanding, the rationale for them seemed to have been that they were preparing sinners for glory. They were not sheer punishment for offenses committed. The "fire" routinely associated with the immediate lot of sinners after death (referred to in 1 Cor 3:10-15) by and large was thought to be purificational fire.

The prayers of the living faithful were seen to be of great value to the dead. People thought they reduced the length of the purificational process. During these years prayers for the dead were introduced into the canon of the Mass. Monasteries and churches retained lists of the dead whose spiritual needs were to be remembered at Mass, especially on the anniversaries of their death. Some Christian writers of the period, such as the English monk Bede (+ 735), spoke more precisely about a place where departed sinners who had repented before death were purified in the afterlife. Unlike hell, residence in this place was temporary. All who "suffer" there are ultimately destined for salvation. In time the place of purgation, which formerly was often thought of as a pit is seen as a "mountain to be scaled," an image that Dante (1265-1321) will immortalize in his famous poem, *Divina Commedia*.

In the eleventh century, a yearly liturgical celebration for the remembrance of departed souls was introduced into the Church calendar by the monastery of Cluny in France. This was All Souls Day, November 2. In short time, this feast of remembrance for the dead was celebrated annually throughout the Church. By the end of the next century (ca. 1170), the term purgatory will be coined. It now occupies a definite place in Catholic thought and teaching, distinct from the two other afterlife destinations, heaven and hell. What until now was considered a process repentant sinners went through becomes a *place* where their purgation happens. It seems the Church after long centuries had arrived at the conclusion that sinners cannot experience the glories of heaven until they have been fully purified of their sins, either in this life through trials and sufferings, or in a purgational place after death. From this time forward the popes, bishops and theologians of the Western Church defended a belief in purgatory against those who would question or deny it. The doctrine, of course, will not be universally accepted. Many will maintain that a person's eternal fate depends entirely on his or her moral status at the time of death. They doubt that corrective or redemptive work of any sort happens in the interim between death and resurrection.

By the thirteenth century, the Western Church settled on a definite geography for life beyond death — the very evil went to hell, the thoroughly good to heaven, and those not fully good or bad to a temporary purgatory for purification, after which they went to heaven. Since arrival of the evil into hell and the thoroughly good into heaven was seen as happening soon after death, there was no "time" delay associated with either. Purgatory, however, seemed to call for some sort of theology of time. These years witnessed something close to mathematical precision about the time-span of purgatory — speculations about ratios between the time one lived in sin before death and the corresponding time that would be needed for purification after death, graver sins deserving greater penances and longer sentences than lesser, etc. Once purgatory received its separate theological geography, the imaginative descriptions of it became even more graphic and lurid.

Efforts were made in this century to reunite the Eastern and Western Churches, which had been separate since 1054. The concept of post-death purification was a part of the reunification discussions. Both Latins and Greeks agreed that some of the dead underwent purification in the afterlife and that prayers of the living were beneficial to them. However, they expressed their beliefs in different ways. The West generally viewed purgatory as needful for the atonement of unrequited sin; the East saw the process more as a purification of the sinner, a period of healing and spiritual growth. For the first time purgatory will be defined as a dogma of the Western Church at the Second Council of Lyons (1274). It was defined again at another reunification council, Florence (1438-1439), and again at Trent (1563).

At Trent, the doctrine of purgatory was defended against the reformers, who denied it outright. They especially objected to what they viewed as the "superstitious" sale of indulgences for the dead. Moreover, they found no biblical or traditional precedent for the doctrine. Though a theological and scriptural case for the granting of indulgences can be made, one must concede the case has not always been well made. The practice is based on the assumed availability to believers of the common treasury of meritorious prayers and good works of the faithful — the Communion of Saints — for the spiritual needs of all, especially for the expiation of sin. Hopefully theologians will some day speak of indulgences in ways that will be understandable to the modern mind.

From the time of the Second Council of Lyons onward, purgatory became an officially accepted truth of faith. Most Catholics accepted the doctrine as true and believable and it became a frequent subject of the sermons of the period. The doctrine spread quickly among the people through the popular preaching of the mendicant orders. These sermons were usually enlivened with edifying stories and legends about dead souls appearing to people seeking their prayers to assist them in the work of their purification. These stories embodied the "need" for purgatory. They made the point that purgatory had to do with the full forgiveness of the repented sins of the dead together with the expiation of sin's evil effects. It was necessary preparation for the vision of God. Souls undergoing this temporary process were in spiritual union with the living. In this purifying work, therefore, the living could assist the dead by their prayers, good works and remembrances at Mass.

In the fourteenth century Dante Alighieri (1265-1321) composed his magnificent poem *Divina Commedia*, in which he describes the three stations of the afterlife. As the Church promoted the existence and purpose of purgatory in her sermons, writings, and official pronouncements, Dante's powerful poem instilled an acceptance of the concept in the minds and hearts of the people. In memorable form, Dante expresses the best theological thought and speculation that had evolved over many centuries in defense of purgatory. He expresses its fundamental meaning and purpose with great nobility and eloquence and brings to the subject a deep and appealing spirituality.

Dante gives purgatory the sensible and attractive image of a mountain. As repentant sinners make their way up its slopes, they are more and more cleansed of their faults and selfishness. When they finally reach the summit, they are fully purified and ready for eternal happiness:

> I raised my eyes in wonder to that mountain that soars high to the heavens . . . higher than sight the peak soared up to the sky.

> Here souls purge themselves of guilt and prepare for their ascent to heaven. . . . Their sufferings cleanse them . . . and straighten out in them what the world has bent.

Since sins diminish the love souls should have for God, the purgatorial climb seeks to restore the love sin destroys:

> The love which in life was lost is paid for and restored.

Dante draws a clear distinction between purgatory and hell:

> Ah, what a difference there is between its
> [purgatory's] paths, and those of hell. Here every
> entrance fills with joyous song, there with sav-
> age cries.

As one proceeds up the mountain, the trip becomes easier;
Dante's guide bids him:

> Come, the stairs are near and now the way up
> the mountain is easier.

The poet sees a reciprocity of spiritual support between the
living and the dead:

> If they [the souls in purgatory] speak our good
> above, we below in our love for God should surely
> help those souls grow cured of time's deep stains,
> so that each at last may issue spotless and unim-
> peded for his starry sphere.

At the summit of the mountain, and at the conclusion of
his vision of purgatory's purifying ordeal, Dante finally
views the "splendor of eternal living light." Indeed, he feels
that his own soul has been purged, "pure and ready to climb
up to the stars." Though it is extremely painful for the soul,
there is a purifying joy to Dante's purgatory. We find much
hope and love here as we move with him progressively upward toward God, his eternal light and glory.

Purgatory retained a substantial place in Catholic thought
and practice from the fourteenth through much of the twen-
tieth century. Through her many avenues of communica-
tion — schools, preaching, books, painting, architecture,
sculpture, religious symbols, stories, etc. — the Church successfully promulgated the doctrine. Remembrance of the spiritual needs of the dead became an essential mark of Catholic

devotion and spirituality. As the living assisted the dead with whom they were spiritually joined, they came to believe that the dead, through their purifying sufferings, could afford spiritual help to them. As believers had always sought the intercession of the saints for their spiritual needs, so they sought the prayerful assistance of the souls in purgatory. The communion of spiritual support between believers, living and dead, became truly reciprocal.

Though today many hold no strong belief in purgatory, it remains a doctrine of faith and this intermediate state continues to have special meaning for many Catholics. They find the doctrine contains several truths of lasting value.

It must be granted, however, that purgatory in its slow and gradual evolution from gospel inference to Catholic dogma, was conceived and spoken of in very exaggerated terms and speculatively described in the severest of images. Unfortunately, the images attached to it and the reasons given to explain and justify it cause many believers to have questions about it. Purgatory needs a theology more in tune with contemporary Christian thought, one that helps believers develop a deeper and more meaningful spirituality.

Chapter 3

• ⌒ •

Is Purgatory Still a Reasonable Belief?

Looking back at this brief review of purgatory's evolution, what can we point to that continues to have spiritual value for Christians today? What elements in purgatory's development call for reform? How can we best rethink the "why" of purgatory?

The Core Doctrine of Purgatory

First, the doctrine gives expression to a concern Christians have instinctively felt for those they know and love who have died. Though Christians devoutly wished that all deceased believers were in heaven with Christ, there was a feeling that because many lived their lives as Christians all too imperfectly, there could well be a delay in their reaching Christ. Most Christians admit their own unworthiness to be so easily and automatically "with the Lord" at death. Thus, they have always shown some uncertainty about those they love. Christians have never thought it strange to pray for their dead. They have done this from the beginning. They felt impelled to assist them as they made their final ascent to God. So, in a sense, purgatory says that to get to heaven "we all need each other." Since we are all in a spiritual union with Christ and prayed for one another in life, it is only natural that we do so in death. Surely our dead remember us; we should remember them.

Secondly, purgatory spells out a profound understanding of the nature of sin that was acquired over years of reflection and introspection. When we sin we knowingly violate God's express will; we break his laws revealed to us either in our natures or in his Scriptures. To sin is to affront his justice and righteousness. It says, in effect, that God and his will are not important to us. Sins also injure the sinner. They cause selfishness to grow deeper roots in the soul. They do spiritual harm to others. We know Christ can and wants to forgive sinners who repent and resolve to avoid their sins in the future. But what about the damage we do ourselves and others because of our selfishness? Should not these "effects" be addressed and repaired for by loving acts, works of selflessness? Sorrow for sin is not the only prerequisite for forgiveness. Christians concluded that more was needed — a willingness to do penance and reparation. This was to act responsibly. It showed our sorrow to be truly genuine.

Since all of us are sinners, part of our earthly task is to work to overcome the damage our sins do. To worry little about them, to do small penance and restorative work for their repair, is to reveal the shallowness and incompleteness of our lives. Since penance is the handmaiden of genuine sorrow, we reveal how lacking in sorrow we are if we ignore or disregard it. If many die having given small effort to the repair of their sins, will God disregard their shallowness? Will he look on them as sufficiently prepared for the joys of heaven as is? Will he say: "Not to worry; the imperatives of the gospel are not as serious as I made them out to be; you died in faith; that's enough for me — take your place in my kingdom?"

Christians, reflecting on the demands of the gospel and the halfhearted way some lived it, concluded that God is unlikely to adopt such a relaxed attitude toward sin. They had serious doubts about the eternal fate of the imperfect believer. Few thought God would deprive them of ultimate salvation. But the gospel says that entrance into heaven is not easily attained. Life has a purpose — to prepare for an eternity with God. If people die having failed to prepare themselves, it follows logically that the task remains to be done. And so the idea of purgatory emerges as a possible answer to Christian concern for the lot of imperfect believers. It does not presume to add things to the gospel that are not there, nor does it contradict anything that is there. It seems to flow logically from the revelation of the gospel, which states over and over again that salvation, though a free gift of God, is something one must seek and prepare oneself for. God wills all to have salvation. If so, he must offer all the opportunity to ready themselves for it. If many die insufficiently ready, it would seem that God, in his mercy, would grant them a chance to dispose themselves finally for glory.

The main burden of spiritual preparation in this intermediate state of purification would obviously fall on the dead themselves. However, the living felt it their duty to assist them in their final preparative ordeal. Thus the practice of offering prayers and good works for their spiritual support became popular, and remembrance of the dead at Mass became a common practice.

At first, there were no defined doctrines or detailed tenets of faith that gave expression to belief in an intermediate state for the dead. They arose as Christians reflected on the gospel. It was simply a matter of making logical assumptions. The belief in purgatory was the offspring of hope, a product of the Christian subconscious. This Christian assumption and practice preceded the definition of the dogma in the late Middle Ages and beyond.

Why did Christians see a need for a state like purgatory? Was it only because they saw an angry God demanding full payment for people's sins?

It is true that many people do see purgatory that way. Believers must be purged and cleansed from all the remnants of sin before gaining access to the presence of God. But other reflective Christians see another purpose for the intermediate state — a place that's needed to complete the task that life on earth was designed to do. The purpose of human life is to prepare oneself to share the selfless love of God eternally. To be ready for this, we must learn how to be selfless in our love of God and others. It is obvious that many die without having gained great facility in loving others selflessly. God in his mercy must help them learn this way of loving. This will not be easy, for learning to love selflessly is never easy.

Is learning to love this way really the purpose of life? Jesus, of course, is the exemplar of selfless love, and much of the New Testament points to this as our real goal. Perhaps no passage speaks more eloquently about it than Paul's hymn to love in 1 Corinthians:

> If I speak in human and angelic tongues but do not have love, I am a resounding gong or a clashing cymbal. And if I have the gift of prophecy and comprehend all mysteries and all knowledge; if I have all faith so as to move mountains but do not have love, I am nothing. If I give away everything I own, and if I hand my body over so that I may boast but do not have love, I gain nothing.
> Love is patient, love is kind. It is not jealous, or

pompous It is not inflated or rude, nor does it seek its own interests. It is not quick-tempered, nor does it brood over injury. It does not rejoice over wrongdoing, but rejoices with the truth. It bears all things, believes all things, hopes all things, endures all things. Love never fails. If there are prophecies, they will be brought to nothing; if tongues, they will cease; if knowledge, it will be brought to nothing.

For now we know partially and we prophesy partially, but when the perfect comes, the partial will pass away. When I was a child, I used to talk as a child, think as a child, reason as a child; when I became a man, I put aside childish things. At present we see indistinctly, as in a mirror, but then face to face. At present I know partially; then I shall know fully, as I am fully known. So faith, hope, love remain, these three; but the greatest of these is love (1 Cor 13).

Heaven is a place for selfless lovers; only they can be at home there. Thus, some "purgatorial" schooling in the art of loving selflessly seems a reasonable expectation for those who die lacking a maturity in this kind of love. Though they are delayed for a time in the intermediate state, these souls are all destined for heaven. There is no despair or bitterness here. Like Advent, the process is grounded in hope; it is a time of anticipated joy.

It must be admitted, however, that as the concept of purgatory evolved, there were several regrettable developments in the way it was explained and described. The images used to depict what went on there were extremely graphic and very exaggerated, and the theologies put forward to justify its existence and purpose were often less than satisfying. Earlier, simpler, less sophisticated Christians might feel at home with such imagery and theology, but as believers became more philosophical and reflective these aspects caused many to wonder whether a place like purgatory was necessary at all.

For example, from Augustine's time the idea of a post-death place for purification was spoken of in heavily legalistic and juristic terms. Sins were seen as crimes or offenses against God's law and these crimes had to be punished. Inordinate stress was given to purgatory as a place of punishment. For each sin there was seen to be a proportionate and fitting penalty. The torments suffered by sinners were like those imagined for the damned — the only difference being that they did not last forever. Because Paul's text, 1 Corinthians 3:10-15, was so often used to give a biblical base for belief in purgatory, the image of fire became its most common simile and many saw this fire in a physical, literal sense. The feeling was that sinners must be completely cleansed before they are allowed to see God. Only the totally pure could share in his holiness. His justice and righteousness demand this.

It is true, of course, that a severe and painful purgatory had salutary effects for the living, eliciting as it did a more serious attitude toward sin, but we can wonder if such a forbidding picture captured the deepest meaning of purgatory. Does God seek full payment for the injuries we do to him and others? Is he so jealous of his holiness that he keeps it from all but the most pure? Fearful of his absolute goodness, did we lose sight of his great mercy and love? Had we forgotten that Scripture speaks of his servant as one who took on himself our sins and suffered for them (Is 52-53; 1 Tm 2:6)? Are there other and deeper reasons why God in his love would see a need for delaying some of his creatures in death before welcoming them into his presence? Has the Spirit revealed all we need to know about purgatory and its purpose, or have we still much to learn about why such a process would fit naturally into the saving plans of a loving God?

Toward a Contemporary Theology of Purgatory

With such questions in mind, we now offer some modest suggestions for a theology of purgatory that could perhaps have more meaning for contemporary Christians.

First, we should recall the theological premises that gave rise to Catholic belief in purgatory. Our discussion of this doctrine must always begin with God. He is the ultimate source of all reality, the creator of all that is. He creates the human soul — it is spiritual, immortal, and free. Though souls live in a material body that ultimately dies, they survive death and live on in a spiritual state in an afterlife. Since God creates the soul, he does so with a plan and purpose in mind. This purpose is revealed in Scripture. There he informs incarnated souls that he wishes them to live their earthly lives in a way that will prepare them to share his love forever — this love is their eternal destiny.

God gives human beings this freedom because he seeks their love; it must be freely given, not forced or programmed. Our love is ours to give or refuse. To respond as God would have us do is not an easy thing, but he promises to help us respond as we should. To refuse love is to sin. It is destructive of life's purpose and frustrates the soul from reaching and sharing God's love. Souls who fall into sin can find forgiveness by coming to Christ penitently. Jesus' forgiveness and strength are God's way of keeping human spirits on the right track to ultimate fulfillment.

How do creatures give their love to God? He tells them that they do this by extending selfless love and service to others.

> Whoever wishes to be great among you will be your servant; whoever wishes to be first among you will be the slave of all (Mk 10:43-44).

> Do to others whatever you would have them do to you (Mt 7:12).

Every good tree bears good fruit (Mt 7:17).

I have given you a model to follow, so that as I have done for you, you should also do (Jn 13:15).

You are my friends if you do what I command you. . . . Go and bear fruit that will remain. . . . This I command you: love one another (Jn 15: 14, 16-17).

Owe nothing to anyone, except to love one another; for the one who loves another has fulfilled the law (Rom 13:8).

If I . . . do not have love, I am a resounding gong . . . I am nothing . . . love is patient, love is kind. It is not jealous or pompous. It is not inflated or rude . . . [it] rejoices with the truth . . . [it] endures all things. Love never fails. . . . So faith, hope, love remain . . . but the greatest of these is love (1 Cor 13).

A life lived in love of others not only results in our being authentic creatures, loved and blessed by God and by those we love. He informs us that such a "giving response" on our part leads to a life where we share his love forever. Life on earth, then, leads to something much grander yet to come. It is a preface to glory, a time of preparation for it.

Could we arrive at glory any other way? Could God perhaps grant it to us in the act of creating us?

Apparently not. To know and be a part of his glory, and for it to be the absolute fulfillment and completion of our being, we need to live out a created life on earth in the way he reveals to us. This is so not only because he wants us freely to choose the glory he offers us — he cannot force it upon us. But also because we must want, seek and be open to it. To be fulfilling, glory can come only where mutual giving and receiving take place. On earth, people dispose and prepare themselves for the glory he offers them. If there is no preparation, disposition, no developed aptitude or receptive capacity for the glory he wants for us, it can never enter, take root, and grow to complete fullness within us This is what "being saved" means. It means God wants to share with creatures his eternal love. The selfless love we share with other human beings is the most beautiful reality we can experience on earth. But not even so wonderful a thing as that can compare in any way to the joy that will come to us in the possession of God's love.

St. Paul assures believers God wants to ". . . pour forth his love into their hearts through the Holy Spirit" (Rom 5:5). But not even God's love can enter and fulfill us if there is no openness or room for it. That's what life is about. It's about making room for the love of God in one's heart. One prepares for the eternal influx of God's love by loving others selflessly. This is life's main purpose. Creatures have a "lifetime" to accomplish this purpose and then they die.

Death is obviously a milestone-moment for us as creatures. It is then that God will judge whether we have accomplished life's purpose or not, whether we have prepared ourselves for an eternal sharing of his love. It seems to me that this is what the judgment that follows death will be about. God will be looking not mainly at the countless stupidities and moral failures we have accumulated during a lifetime; he will be looking at our "hearts." With all our sins, is there still some room there for him?

And the outcome of this judgment? Before the time of Christ, no one could precisely define it. With Jesus, the aftermath of judgment becomes much clearer. Resurrection of the body and heaven are in store for those who lived their lives correctly after the pattern he gave us. Hell or damnation awaits those who in an absolute way reject God and the saving message he gives us in Christ.

If Christians can accept the foregoing premises as a reasonable interpretation of what God has told them about life's purpose, a question, then, can legitimately be raised: What happens to a soul that dies with a mixed record of good and evil while on earth? What about those who never reject God in a total and absolute way, but who follow him only with half-hearted love and commitment? They may be blessed with God's forgiveness at death, but their state of preparation for sharing in the selfless love of God can only be described as disappointing and imperfect. Their lives were more selfish than selfless. Their sins compounded their self-centeredness. They did harm to others which largely went unheeded and unrepaired. Is there room for such people in one or other of the two destinations mentioned above — heaven or hell?

Revelation speaks clearly of these two eternal "places." But is it not reasonable to assume there might be a temporary third "place" between the two poles where souls inadequately prepared for glory can finally do what is necessary to prepare them for heaven?

Scripture not only exhorts people to live and die as believers. It tells them it is important that they live their lives properly. The living well is not incidental to his will and purpose. It has to do with proper preparation for what awaits them. If there is not enough serious attention to this, it stands to reason that a need for further preparation will face these souls after death. And would not God, willing the salvation of all, provide all of his creatures the means of realizing this salvation? If it so turns out that he finds insufficient space in the hearts of some for his love, would not the possibility of a temporary purgatory as a place finally to learn selflessness be a merciful answer? To admit any and all into paradise without preparation would be for God to negate the demands of his own gospel.

Whoever wishes to come after me must deny himself, take up his cross, and follow me. For whoever wishes to save his life will lose it, but whoever loses his life for my sake and that of the gospel will save it (Mk 8:34-35).

So be perfect, just as your heavenly Father is perfect (Mt 5:48).

For the Son of Man will come with his angels in his Father's glory, and then he will repay everyone according to his conduct (Mt 16:27).

Those who have done good deeds will rise to the resurrection of life, but those who have done wicked deeds will rise to the resurrection of condemnation (Jn 5:29).

You are my friends if you do what I command you. . . . Go and bear fruit that will remain. . . . Love one another (Jn 15:14, 16-17).

Do you not know that the unjust will not inherit the kingdom of God (1 Cor 6:9).

For we must all appear before the judgment seat of Christ, so that each one may receive recompense, according to what he did in the body, whether good or evil (2 Cor 5:10).

The do's and don'ts in the gospel were not designed just to make life difficult and to test the depth of people's discipleship. They were the "how-to" instructions that each one must follow to reach the fullness of divine love. They inform people what they must do to reach heaven. Jesus, the human Jesus especially, was God's premier instructor. And like good instructors, he not only clearly taught believers the acts that would lead them to God. In his life he showed them the acts that must be done to reach God. He is Savior. He is also the model of how one becomes fully assimilated into the love of the Savior.

Jesus: Model as Well as Savior

Among New Testament writers, St. Paul perhaps more clearly than others sees the human Jesus as the supreme model of how one reaches the fullness of God's love. This is particularly illustrated in the hymn to Christ he quotes in his letter to the Philippians, chapter 2, verses 6 to 11. He presents the human Jesus as a model of humility that the Philippians should imitate.

> Who, though he was in the form of God,
> did not regard equality with God something to be
> grasped.
>
> Rather, he emptied himself,
> taking the form of a slave,
> coming in human likeness;
> and found human in appearance,
>
> he humbled himself,
> becoming obedient to death,
> even death on a cross.
> Because of this, God greatly exalted him
> and bestowed on him the name
> that is above every name,
> that at the name of Jesus
> every knee should bend,
> of those in heaven and on earth and under the
> earth,

and every tongue confess that
Jesus Christ is Lord,
to the glory of God the Father (Phil 2:6-11).

How did Jesus acquire Resurrection and exaltation? As man, how did he experience a full sharing in God's glory? Why was he given the Name above all names — that of Lord? The hymn says it was because of the self-emptying (*kenosis*) quality and character of his life and death. Given great gifts and powers by God, he did not cling to them selfishly. He gave them all away in the service of others, and did so throughout his life all the way to his death on the cross. So it could be said that at the end he died totally empty. In a sense, it would appear in his "emptiness" he dies a failure, devoid of anything good for himself. But is a life of self-emptying service for others a failure?

The answer is clearly shown in God's reaction and response to the cross — Jesus' final act of self-emptying. That which is completely empty of self can then be totally filled with God's love and glory.

The point is eloquently made. To reach and be filled with God's love, we must empty ourselves of our gifts and powers in the service of others. Jesus teaches us how to do it. The more we give away, the more we will receive. In eternal terms there is no other way. If we die largely filled with self, how can God fill us with his love? In sad reality, we leave him no room.

Is it not reasonable to assume that many die believers, repentant of their sins, but still more selfish than they should be? The task of earthly life has only partially been done. More *kenosis* effort on their part seems in order. In such instances, a purgatory of some sort would seem a way life's *kenosis* work can be completed. In this view, purgatory would not so much be "punishment" for past sins as a process in which the dead can purify themselves of the selfishness that remains in them.

Heaven is not delayed because they've suffered too little for their sins; it's delayed because there is not yet room in their hearts for the incoming love of God.

When we keep the Philippian hymn in mind as we read the letters of Paul, it will be easier to understand why he led the self-sacrificing life he did, and why he could even rejoice in his sufferings (Col 1:24). Before his conversion, Paul doubtless looked at Jesus as a lawless, deceiving preacher, whose awful death must have been God's punishment for his deceit and blasphemies. But after he encountered the Christ of glory, Paul realized that what looked like God's disapproval and punishment was in fact the last *kenosis* act of Christ — the act in which he fully gave himself for others.

Paul could see that Christ was filled with all of God's love because he gave himself to death in such heroic measure. His Resurrection and exaltation make manifest that such was the case. If a *kenosis*-like life is the sure way to God and glory, then Paul understood that he must model his life after that of Christ. He too must live a *kenosis*-like life in the service of others. This is why he works so tirelessly for Christ. He is not rejoicing because he literally enjoys hard work and pain. He rejoices because he knows that only in the giving of himself can he be filled with what he desires above all — the fullness of God's love.

Before conversion Paul probably thought that his zealous observance of the law was his ticket to glory and paradise; he had to accumulate credits, pious acts and good works in order to earn a place in heaven. Now he sees clearly that paradise is beyond earning; it is realized by disposing and preparing himself for its sure "incoming" at death. It will profit him little if he ends up filled with "credits." What he must end up with is a heart empty of self, an emptiness that God will infallibly fill with his love. The same can be said for all the saints and martyrs in Christian history. They were presumed to be in heaven. Why? Their preparation was manifestly done. Their total commitment to Christ was not in doubt; they were selfless people who cared about the needs of others. We remember them in prayer to thank God for their lives and to seek their intercession.

It is others we pray for — the less-than-saintly whose preparation is incomplete. It is not that we think God loves them less. It is their moral failures, their ambiguous commitment. These cause us to worry about their readiness to be with God.

Do Christians have a theological base for believing the saints are surely with God while the imperfect quite likely are still in transit toward him? Yes — the gospel message itself!

Time and again it stated that there is a causal connection between what people do with their lives on earth and the reaching of God in heaven (see again such texts as: Mk 8:34-35; Mt 5:48; 16:27; Jn 5:29; 15:14; 1 Cor 6:9-10; 2 Cor 5:10). It would be easy to put the eternal fate of the dead completely in God's hands, to let him take care of all the problems. But instinctively Christians worried about their dead, because the gospel gave them cause to worry. It clearly stated the hereafter depends on the life one lives before death. Moreover, as noted earlier, Christians knew death did not separate them from the dead. Their common faith in Christ made them spiritually one with each other. As Christians need the support and prayers of fellow believers during their lifetimes, this need continues in death. And as Christians thought of their dead who died with faults and weaknesses, they knew these departed souls sought their help to repair and make up for their acts of selfishness, their less than perfect response to God. In addition, Christians knew they had a powerful ally to help the dead make atonement for their sins — Jesus himself. He died to overcome the sins of all. Thus people sought to include the spiritual needs of the dead in his atoning sacrifice, and did so by remembering them at Mass.

Chapter 4

Reflections on Common Objections to Purgatory

Is God This Demanding?

Some object to the doctrine of purgatory because it implies a harsh and punitive God. Others say that a "sentence" in such a place of pain and suffering would be so crushing and burdensome that a person would prefer permanent death or annihilation rather than undertake it.

Such objections can be seen as a response to an older conception of purgatory. The imaginative speculations of Christians in the early and later Middle Ages depicted purgatory as extremely painful and frightening. Sins were seen primarily as violations of God's goodness and purity. They made sinners impure in his sight, unworthy to live in his presence. This "impurity" had to be removed by the cleansing "fire" of God.

As fire purifies the dross elements in metal, so it was thought God must cleanse the soul from the corrupting effects of sin with his "purifying fire."

The old images too easily educe pictures of literal physical pain as the means of purification. In our more sophisticated age, purgatory obviously needs some new imagery. Perhaps the "pains and sufferings" could be better described as psychological and spiritual. They have to do with the educational process at the heart of purgatory's purpose — making a person more selfless and open to God. Certainly that is not an easy or painless thing to accomplish. It is not painless now, in this life. Most likely it would not be painless beyond death. But the difficulties and hardship of undergoing purification would not lead to anxiety or despair. The entire process would be rooted in Christian hope; it would be permeated with a deep sense of anticipated joy.

In her *Treatise on Purgatory*, St. Catherine of Genoa (1447-1510), a mystic, says that the only joy greater than the joy of the souls in purgatory is that of the saints in paradise. She says that as the residue of their sins and selfishness gradually disappears, the souls in purgatory grow steadily in happiness as God's love flows into their souls. Through the purifying process they are gaining facility in their ability to love selflessly.

Dante and the Christian mystics were probably close to the truth when they spoke of purgatory, despite its many pains and sufferings, as a school of virtue, a learning and maturing experience. God is in the process. His transforming graces are helping these souls become what they need to become. Heaven is very close and those being purified would know they are ultimately destined to arrive there.

God Doesn't Need Purgatory

Some object that purgatory is unnecessary. This earthly life is sufficient for God's purposes.

However, doesn't this objection actually set limits on God's power over evil? It asserts that God's ability to save people ends with their death. When they die, their fate is sealed. Death is the cut-off point beyond which no changes or reforms can take place. Yet the plain fact known to all is that many of God's creatures die with elements of evil still part of their makeup. Is the all-powerful, all-loving God now powerless to overcome these remnants of evil?

Christian eschatology clearly proclaims the opposite. It states that God will conquer all evil — especially "at the end." Christian eschatology identifies Jesus as the "destroyer of all evil" (2 Thes 2:8). Why, then, confine his role as the "destroyer" to temporal, pre-death history? He is the merciful Lord of all history the life to come as well as this life. He is eternally Savior, forgiver, purifier, good shepherd, final Adam, head of believers, possessor and grantor of all God's promises. At death, there still seems much in many of us that our eschatological Lord must help us overcome before our entrance into paradise. Those who would confine God's saving activity only to this life would do well to reflect on two passages of Scripture. The first, from Romans, proclaims God's eternal love and his power over death even the physical death of unprepared believers:

> What then shall we say to this? If God is for us, who can be against us? He who did not spare his own Son, but handed him over for us all, how will he not give us everything else along with him? Who will bring a charge against God's chosen ones? It is God who acquits us. Who will condemn? It is Christ Jesus who died, rather, was raised, who also is at the right hand of God, who intercedes for us. What will separate us from the love of Christ? Will anguish, or distress, or persecution, or famine, or nakedness, or peril, or the sword? As it is written:

"For your sake we are being slain all the day;
we are looked upon as sheep to be slaughtered."

No, in all these things we will conquer completely through him who loved us. For I am con-
vinced that neither death, nor life, nor angels, nor
principalities, not things present, nor things to
come, no powers, not height, or depth, or any other
creature will be able to separate us from the love
of God in Christ Jesus our Lord (Rom 8:31-39).

The second passage, from 1 Timothy, is one we cited earlier. It declares God's resolve to save *everyone*:

This is good and pleasing to God our savior,
who wills everyone to be saved and to come to
knowledge of the truth. For there is one God.
There is also one mediator between God and the
human race, Christ Jesus, himself human, who
gave himself as ransom *for all* (1 Tm 2:3-6).

Is it not, therefore, reasonable for people to believe that God's
battle with evil does not cease at the grave? It continues beyond
death as long as there remains a spark of savability in a soul. In
past times when Christians prayed fervently for their dead it
showed they instinctively believed that God continued his saving work with those who died not fully prepared for him.

Purgatory Lacks Biblical Foundation

The lack of explicit description of purgatory in Scripture
is not proof that no such place exists. Much that Christians
believe is not explicitly described in Scripture. The doctrine
of the Trinity, for example, is nowhere mentioned there. Like
many other Christian beliefs, it has scriptural support, but was
formulated over time, as Christians reflected on God's revelation of himself.

Scripture is not a treatise on the afterlife. It is aimed at the living. It is the living who are to listen to God, hear his gospel, obey it, do it. If there is meager listening, obeying and doing, then the dead will learn the full consequences of such failure when they die. Besides, foreknowledge of further chances for the selfish would only compound the numbers of the unprepared.

Indeed, the need for purgatory is often inferred in Scripture. When Christians believe in purgatory they are not going beyond the gospel. On the contrary, they show they take seriously its insistence that life is a preparation for God's love. This love comes to those who are disposed for it. It cannot be decreed by God or granted whether people are disposed for it or not. Scripture is clear on this point:

> Whoever wishes to come after me must deny himself, take up his cross, and follow me. For whoever wishes to save his life will lose it, but whoever loses his life for my sake and that of the gospel will save it (Mk 8:34-35).

> So be perfect, just as your heavenly Father is perfect (Mt 5:48).

> For the Son of Man will come with his angels in his Father's glory, and then he will repay everyone according to his conduct (Mt 16:27).

> The hour is coming in which all who are in the tombs will hear his voice and will come out, those who have done good deeds will rise to the resurrection of life, but those who have done wicked deeds will rise to the resurrection of condemnation (Jn 5:28-29).

Do you not know that the unjust will not inherit the kingdom of God? (1 Cor 6:9).

For we must all appear before the judgment seat of Christ, so that each one may receive recompense, according to what he did in the body, whether good or evil (2 Cor 5:10).

The gospel says that the good, the selfless and loving go to heaven; the bad to hell. Some, therefore, might too readily conclude that this rules out a third possibility, purgatory. But again, we must ask some questions: Is anyone's life so clearly good or bad that a determination of placement can easily be made at the moment of physical death? Can any of us speak with certitude about what happens after death? Can we unequivocally say that all further opportunities to prepare oneself for God cease completely?

Death could very well be a time of new and illuminating insights where life's purpose is brought home to the dead with a clarity never realized before. The vital importance of preparing ourselves for intimacy with God could at last become convincingly clear to us. With this new awareness, the desire to do what is necessary would be intensely felt. Would God be any less intense in his desire to offer the imperfect a chance at final preparation? A God who wills salvation for all would offer all the means to that end.

Purgatory Is More Pelagian Than Christian

Some detect a whiff of the Pelagian heresy in the doctrine of purgatory — the notion that human beings can earn or in some way deserve their salvation. Purgatory, they say, compromises or competes with Jesus' role as Savior. Salvation is seen as completely and exclusively his work. The only essential task for creatures is to submit to Christ in faith. When that is done, God pretty much takes over and does the rest. He embraces and forgives believers, purifies and prepares them, assures them they will end up in heaven. Purgatory dangerously resembles Pelagianism, for it says no one gets to heaven or glory without doing the "preparation thing." Purgatory seems to say that believers "earn" their salvation by living in a certain way.

No, belief in purgatory does not say that at all. Salvation is the freely bestowed love of God; only he can give it. Purgatory is an inference from what the gospel proclaims — people experience salvation when they hear the gospel and respond to it (Lk 11:28). Jesus can only save those who seek his salvation; they must be open to it, disposed to receive it. The imperatives of the gospel contain many do's and don'ts. These are all aimed at making hearers of the gospel receptive to the love of God in Christ. This love exists beyond and outside of ourselves. Thus we must strive to become outward, other-directed people, open to the needs of others. The gospel says that we find and serve God when we get out of ourselves, when we love and serve others in a selfless way. He locates himself there to draw us more and more out of ourselves and toward him.

The thrust of the imperatives of the gospel do not come naturally to us. Most of us are more drawn to acts of self-satisfaction than selfless other-directed actions. But in essence the gospel states that life's fundamental task is to become more and more empty of self — for only the empty can be filled. And if we end a lifetime filled too much with self, the love of God cannot find easy entrance.

Those who say that purgatory implies that we can earn our salvation would do better to ask whether God would abandon the selfish dead. Would a God who wills the salvation of all write anyone off, especially if he finds in them minimum residues of faith and openness? But we must take him at his word. He cannot disregard the need for people to do what he said was essential to do: "For whoever wishes to save his life will lose it, but whoever loses his life for my sake and that of the gospel will save it" (Mk 8:35). The selfish dead have done too little "giving of their lives." They must die to self in service of others. This is what will open them to the life and love of God.

Purgatory will be about completing the process of "dying to self." This should have been done before death. If not done, it seems logical and plausible that in God's mercy it be done after death. To say that the "the dying to self" cannot continue after death is to put limits on God that no one should ever presume to place:

> What then are we to say? Is there injustice on the part of God? Of course not! For he says to Moses:
> "I will show mercy to whom I will,
> I will take pity on whom I will."
> So it depends not upon a person's will or exertion, but upon God, who shows mercy. . . . Consequently, he has mercy upon whom he wills (Rom 9:14-18).

No one can be certain how the "dying to self" takes place in purgatory and for how long. This has not been revealed. But taking into account the moral condition of the world, the relativistic attitudes about right and wrong that prevail, the smugness, pride, complacency, the self-absorption of so many, one must conclude that many die far short of accomplishing what the gospel asks of them. Some might see the fate of such people as hopeless, but surely God does not. His will is to save. Until he finds total self-absorption or complete rejection, he would continue in his resolve to save the dead.

A Vindictive God?

Powerful objections to purgatory are fueled by the distaste many feel for the harsh picture the doctrine gives of God. A

God who demands so much suffering and atonement for sins committed could be regarded as more vindictive than merciful and loving. If Christ forgave the thief who was crucified with him and assured him he would be in paradise that day (Lk 23:43), why would he delay others and subject them to the "torments" of purgatory? And besides, does Scripture not say that Jesus himself is the main expiation and atonement for all sin (Rom 3:25)? Far better to believe in a God of mercy, love and tolerance than a God who demands so much.

This is a reaction to an earlier understanding of purgatory as a "place" of punishment, where people paid the full price for a sinful life. Many of these harsh images of God's reaction to sin and sinners that unfortunately became attached to the concept of purgatory derive from Old Testament descriptions of Yahweh as a jealous God calling for the blood of sinners, demanding sacrifices, vengeance, etc. Where ancient writers quite likely intended the images to be metaphorical commentary on the seriousness of sin, people in time took the images as the literal reaction of God to sin. The equal emphasis in the Old Testament on the mercy and love of God and his willingness to forgive sinners should have alerted them to understand these frightening images as human attempts to promote serious respect for God's goodness and holiness, while at the same time motivating people to avoid sin.

Too strong an emphasis on purgatory as punishment is perhaps the wrong way to look at it. God is not trying to "get even" with people, nor is purgatory his way of lowering the boom. In its deepest meaning the doctrine says that God is mercifully preparing unprepared creatures for the joys of heaven. They were charged by the gospel to prepare for heaven while alive on earth. He extended graces to help them prepare for these joys countless times. If people gave small notice to him and prepared much less seriously than they should have, do they not thereby find themselves at death in an uncertain and precarious position? Whose fault is that?

Purgatory says that God does not regard this failure as final. He does not come to us and say, "You've failed me completely. Enough! I'm through with you!" Rather, he comes to help us complete the work we've left undone. The pains, punishment, torment, "fire" used to describe the final purifying process are not literal pictures of what purgatory will be like. These were just graphic metaphors to teach the lesson that heaven is not easily acquired. It is "taken by violence" in the sense that one's absorption with self is not easy to give up. A "dying to self," a *kenosis*, must take place before full assimilation into God's love can happen. The *kenosis* undertaken by the human Jesus was not an easy task for him, and our *kenosis* will not be easy either.

The how of one's post-death *kenosis* is matter for speculation only because Scripture has little to say about how this spiritual work will be done. It would seem more than likely, however, that one's final purification will take place in and with a community of "others" undergoing similar purification. Interaction with the human family was God's planned context for our becoming more selfless while on earth. It would follow that interaction with other souls in the intermediate state of purgatory would provide the optimum context for acquiring the openness and selflessness the unprepared lack. Souls in final transition to God can give of themselves in prayer and works for the needs of others. And, of course, these souls are joined spiritually to members of the body of Christ still making the earthly pilgrimage. These members need the prayers and support of fellow Christians as they learn how to live the gospel. Souls in purgatory can be of spiritual help to them. As the living can help and support the dead by prayers and good works, so the dead can assist the living. Certainly those still living who may have suffered ill effects from the sins of the dead can find comfort and solace in the repentant and sorrowing prayers of those who injured them. Thus the souls in purgatory have a vast community toward which they can direct their thoughts and prayers in a selfless way.

Purgatory is not a chamber of horrors. It is a place where shallowness and selfishness are overcome. It is a time of spiritual growth and maturing. It infallibly leads to the vision of God. That vision can be experienced and enjoyed intensely only when one comes to it fully open to God. If he were to put people in heaven selfish, unprepared, and spiritually immature, it could not really be heaven for them. It is in full giving of self that one receives the fullness of God's love. His purpose and end in creating us was his desire to share with us his full love (1 Tm 2:3-6). If so, he will surely provide us the means to receive it. For those insufficiently prepared at death, purgatory would seem his blessed means of doing so.

A Doctrine for the Irresponsible?

Some object that belief in purgatory could make people less serious about life's purpose. If merciful "second chances" can be given in the life to come, why should anyone worry about seriously developing other-directed, selfless attitudes and habits now?

On the contrary, purgatory is not advocated as an alternate easy out for Johnny-come-latelies; it will be far from easy. If few selfless works were done on earth, the compensating works of purgatory will be all the more spiritually difficult. Purgatory is not an option for the cynical, the justifiers of evil, those who grossly abuse the gift of life. There is another option for those who make mockery of God — an eternity without him. Purgatory is for those who were not wholehearted enough in doing what their hearts told them they should do. They died having accomplished part of the work God asked of them, but not all. It is his merciful option for the incomplete, not those who reject him altogether.

Far from encouraging people to live their lives irresponsibly in selfish indulgence, purgatory should motivate them to take life seriously. Life is not a question mark. Its meaning has been revealed. It is an apprenticeship for heaven. The gospel tells us how to get there. No one should ever wish for purgatory. They should aim for heaven and stay on the course that leads them there. Purgatory is a constant reminder that no one reaches God by chance.

Many people, caught up in the joys, sorrows, demands of earthly life, tend to live for the moment, giving little thought to an afterlife and a necessary connection between then and now. But Christianity is premised on an afterlife, and our status and life there will flow inevitably from what we do now. Life is preface to an eternity of happiness and glory. But that will be realized only when we prepare and dispose ourselves for it. If we die more selfish than serving, much of life's work remains still to be done. As Catholics see it, purgatory is where the unfinished business will be done.

Christian history, from an early date, saw something like a post-death purgatory in the picture. Far from being an eccentric belief of a small and uninformed minority, it became generally accepted as a truth of faith. For many it helped to spawn a spirituality of high quality. It not only prompted Christians to continue prayerful remembrance of the spiritual needs of the dead. It worked to motivate them to remain faithful to the imperatives of the gospel. These requirements were given to ready them for glory. An authentic spirituality takes them seriously. As the human Jesus reached glory by living the gospel, so his disciples will arrive there by striving to live as Jesus lived.

In the difficult pressure-filled times of life, people might want a less demanding God and wish for an easier path to glory than the self-giving way of Jesus. But to wish that is to cheapen God and the glory he wants for us. There is only one sure way to reach his glory. Jesus has shown us how. Unless we bring a selfless Christ-like love to God, we will never know how immense and beautiful his love for us is. We reach this love not

simply by enduring life on earth; we obtain it by actively trying to empty and purify ourselves of self in the service of others. God's love is always ready to fill and fulfill us completely.
But this filling can take place only when self-emptiness has
been accomplished. We must accomplish this before we die.
If not, where else but in purgatory?

Chapter 5

Thoughts on the "Final Option"

Some contemporary theologians, perhaps without intending to, have made an intermediate state for the unprepared less necessary by positing the likelihood of a "final option" — a choice for or against God that all will be able to make at death. These theorists say that all will encounter God when they die. In that experience even the unprepared will see clearly the purpose of life and how it should have been lived. They will be made aware of how well or imperfectly they lived it. In this encounter they will be given the chance to straighten things out, to repent all their moral failures. They will be given the opportunity to choose God or reject him. So in a sense the final option theory eclipses the need for an extended period of further preparation for glory.

Certainly one can applaud a theory that underscores the

immensity of God's love and mercy, that shows him desirous to save everyone, to give all of his creatures, the good and the not-so-good, a final chance to choose for or against him. In this hypothesis, death catches no one by surprise. All will be able freely to choose the eternal destiny they desire.

Few Christians would deny that death is an extremely important moment for everyone. Most believe that after death they will encounter God. But this God will not be a stranger to them; they have met him many times spiritually since they first became believers. He called for their faith. They responded to his call and willingly gave their faith to him. For most Christians, the "option" for God is not a rare event. They have opted for God many times. They have heard his message in the Scriptures. They have seen him in the good lives of fellow believers. He was with them in all their crises and sufferings. He heard their prayers and answered them in ways that best suited their spiritual needs. Christians know which acts in their lives please him, which acts disappoint him. They know why God gave them life. He has told them all this in the message he gave them.

In death, God will respect their freedom — as he always does. He will not arbitrarily assign them to this place or that. How they used this freedom, the path and direction in life they have chosen to follow, will be crucial in deciding where they go. Doubtless God will want believers to reconfirm all life's positive options; he will want them to opt for him in this critical moment of death. But Christians come to him with specific histories that sum up their response to him. In his message he told them how important their individual histories were. As they live their lives so they will be judged.

> For the Son of Man will come with his angels in his Father's glory, and then he will repay everyone according to his conduct (Mt 16:27).

> For we must all appear before the judgment seat
> of Christ, so that each one may receive recom-
> pense, according to what he did in the body,
> whether good or evil (2 Cor 5:10).

The time of death is obviously an important and defining moment, but all of a Christian's important pre-death
moments are equally defining. To say the option at death is
what mainly determines our eternal fate is to trivialize one's
earthly history and the gospel message. All of its imperatives were addressed to the *living*. In the gospel, God tells believers over and over again that it is *how they live*, what they
do or don't do *on earth*, that determines what happens when
they die.

If the gospel so emphatically stresses a causal connection between what we do now and our status in the life to
come, an important question arises. Will God's judgment
easily identify who goes where? Are the worthy clearly
identifiable? Are the unworthy obvious and easy to sort
out?

The answer would seem to be that a good number of
those who die come to God in a state of spiritual ambigu-
ity. The saints, of course, would be easy to identify because of
their selfless lives. Their worthiness to enter heaven would be
obvious, and God would quickly draw them into the embrace
of his love. But what of those who were far from saintly, who
in weakness were often sinful, selfish, more wrapped up in
their own wants and desires than the good of others? Many
such people sorrow over their selfishness, their sins of com-
mission and omission. They repent and confess their sinfulness and receive God's forgiveness. Still, they often ignored
God's desire that they live good and selfless lives. As forgiven,
do they thereby take on equal status with the saints? Are they
ready for heaven as is?

No one could ever doubt that God is able to open the heavens to all who repent their sins and believe. But again, we must come back to a key point of revelation — the purpose of life is to prepare ourselves for heaven. God is not powerless or unwilling to save the imperfect. Of course he can save them. He has saved them. That's what the gospel proclaims — all creation is saved by the life, death and Resurrection of Christ. But the gospel also proclaims that people must respond to the Christ who saves. They must accept him as their Savior and live the life he asks them to live. Jesus is not only Savior; he is model. The salvation he offers the world is a grace he bestows, but those who would have it are asked to embrace and pursue a way of life. Heaven is not the inevitable destination of those who seek it; it is something people must prepare and dispose themselves for.

If heaven can be had by anyone who believes, by anyone who simply wishes for it, why are we not created *in* heaven to begin with? The answer seems to be that heaven cannot be heaven unless a person is prepared for and disposed toward it. The gospel is not about faith alone; it is about exercised faith. We must not only believe in Christ; we must follow him and model our lives after the pattern he gave us, living a selfless, loving and serving life — as he did.

If we come to God in death with meager amounts of Christ-like activity to our credit (albeit repentant and forgiven), would not most of us feel ill prepared for and most undeserving of heaven? Our sins and selfishness have left wounding effects on our souls and the souls of others. Forgiveness alone cannot heal that. We must purge the unworthiness that weighs heavily on our spirits for the ill-spent moments of our lives. Heaven is God filling us with his selfless love. The selfishness that remains in us frustrates the coming of his fullness. Further purification and preparation seem in order.

The final option notion is a modern idea. Christians almost from the beginning instinctively prayed for their dead. Clearly, they felt that death did not mean automatic heaven for all believers. Indeed, many of the "faithful departed" could still be pilgrims in the journey toward God. Death did not sever their spiritual union with their loved ones. They prayed for them on earth. They should remember their needs in death.

Chapter 6

Death: A Speculative Scenario

It is time to gather together these reflections on the origins and rationale of the Catholic doctrine of purgatory. Perhaps this can best be done by speculating for a moment on what death might be like for the "average Christian" — that is, a believer whose faith was often lived imperfectly, or as Augustine would say, a person who was good but not all good.[1]

As death occurs, this person realizes that his earthly life is over — that historical chapter is now behind him. However, he is conscious and still feels very much alive. In full realization that there is no possibility of going back, this person natu-

---

[1] To avoid a multiplicity of "hims" and "hers" in this theological speculation, I will refer to the departed person as "him" — understanding that "him" represents all "average believers," male and female.

rally turns his attention and focus to a new future that is opening up for him. He has a sense that he has arrived at a whole
new plateau of personal existence.

Having lived his life in a smaller world of specific persons,
places, situations, occupations, etc., he seems to be moving
toward a much larger world. He is now more conscious that
there is a cosmos beyond his former familiar earthly circum-
stance. He has intimations that this will be his future dwelling
place and he desires to move toward this larger world. He hopes
to be accepted and to feel at home here. He also realizes he is
not yet free to move in that direction before important judg-
ments about him, his life, his earthly history are made. In his
anticipation he feels a nearness to God he has never felt before. He is certain that God is to be the judge who will decide
his cosmic future.

What will be God's main inquiry in this judgment? Since
this person sees most clearly the outlines of his life, who he
was and what he did for good or ill, he knows that God will
be most interested in his moral and spiritual life — the state
of his soul. Has he lived life well and is he spiritually prepared for the new life that lies ahead? Fully realizing his failures and shortcomings, he nevertheless welcomes this judgment. He has the deepest desire to know God's decision on
his future.

He has never experienced such closeness to the ground
of his being before and he feels strongly impelled to come
closer to God and to be loved by him. His mind seems
flooded with many new and revealing insights. He becomes
aware of God's plan that moved him to create the universe.
He sees the place God had for him in this plan, the great
love that permeates every aspect of it. What was vague and
unclear about God before seems now to be coming into
sharper focus. The sheer nearness of God shows him to be
clearly the source and center of all being. Like an overpowering light, God removes from this person every element

of self-delusion and pretense. He knows who and what he truly is, how prepared or unprepared he is for what is to come. He is anxious, and in some ways fearful, but still intensely eager to learn God's verdict on his state of soul.

Then — the encounter! What his faith told him would happen at death, happens. He now sees that life was not a chance temporary event, an opportunity to experience a small taste of aliveness before oblivion. It was a period of interim schooling for something far greater — an eternity of indescribable happiness. His faith informed him that life must be lived properly for him to reach this eternity. It could not be bestowed outright. He must do good actions to render him receptive and disposed for it. After his earthly life he would be judged on how he lived. That moment has now come. God's verdict is about to be given. Did he adequately prepare for eternity, or did he fail to do so? Will God go over in detail the good and bad elements of his life? I rather imagine there will be no need for words or detail. Standing in the presence of God, and flooded with the overpowering light that emanates from him, the condition of one's soul will be all too obvious, not only to God, but to him as well. After all, there can only be one of two verdicts handed down — prepared or unprepared.

The gospel told believers how best to prepare for an eternity with God. The focus of judgment will obviously be on that — did he do what Christ urged him to do; did he do it well enough? Christ wanted us to be people of faith — people who listened openly to his message and accepted it and him as God's Word. In Christ and his revelations we discovered the deepest meaning of life, the ultimate reason for existence, the final destiny toward which all life must move. In faith we must accept him as God's Word, our alpha and omega.

As human beings we were to know good and bad times. We were to experience sorrows along with our joys. Our faith was to be tested often, and so God wanted us to be people of hope, followers who would hang on to our beliefs even in difficult and troubling times through all of life up to the end of it. Through faith and hope we were to accept Christ as our Lord and Savior and enter into a spiritual union with him.

In Christ we were to find the model of how to live human life correctly. We were to be like him — a person who lived completely for others, who loved and served people selflessly. More than all else, Jesus wanted his followers to be people of faith, hope and love. These soul-virtues not only identified us as his disciples; they were the means that best prepared us for our life with him in heaven. Faith brings us to Jesus, hope keeps us there, and selfless love refashions us in his image. Heaven is for Christ-like people. This is what God will be looking for.

Have we come to him bearing a sufficient likeness to the human Christ? He was sent to us not only to talk about God, but to lead us to God. He showed us how to live so that when we got there, we would stay forever. Jesus was a come-to-God, stay-with-God person. So we were to be — that was our main task on earth. In death we now face the critical moment of judgment.

Are we sufficiently prepared for full assimilation into God's love, or have we come to him not yet ready for so wonderful a grace? Will he find us in some way incomplete? The verdict will be rendered. Because our life will be present to us in a summary way, we will know what we did right, what we did wrong. And should the verdict be "not fully prepared" we will know why it is so. We will naturally feel regret over the inadequacy of our record, but there will be no despair or bitterness, for in the verdict, God will make known to us how we can finish the work we sadly left incomplete. Heaven is near and clearly realizable. As we accept God's verdict and embrace the chance he gives us to complete our preparative work, we are consumed with a feeling of confident hope and inner peace.

Since deficiencies in the quality and depth of this person's faith, hope and love were still present at death, his immediate task will be to open his spirit more generously to the acquisition of these three essential virtues. This work can be called "punishment" only in the sense that it will be spiritually and psychologically demanding, as the acquisition of virtue always is.

The continuation and intensification of this work is aimed at his spiritual growth and maturity. The process can also be called "purifying," for through it, with God's help, he will be purging the remnants of selfishness from his heart. He will be developing a more open and serving attitude toward God and others. Thus we continue to call this interim state "purgatory."

As this person becomes progressively more selfless and caring of others, he roots out and cleanses from his soul the stains and imperfections that sin has worked on it. At last he finally realizes that God cannot make him what he must become himself and what his life was given him to become. God cannot be total purifier. The creature must freely participate and do his part.

How long will this process go on? Only as long as needed. This person is here not mainly to satisfy justice. (Who could ever do that adequately?) He is here to ready himself for glory. As much as this person yearns for heaven, God yearns even more strongly to have him there and remains with him through the purifying ordeal.

God promises all believers his eternal love and glory when they arrive at judgment empty of self-love. If this person had only his own efforts to purge the remaining selfishness from his heart, the task would be nearly impossible. But this saving work is accomplished in union with the purifying power of God himself. The final purification of the soul happens because the transforming power of God works in tandem with the repentant sinner. Indeed, living Christians and the saints in heaven are one with him in their prayers and spiritual support helping him in this holy work. When this "work" is done, heaven will open wide to welcome him. He will recognize at last that God excludes no one from paradise. Only individual creatures can exclude themselves, or, through lack of seriousness and proper preparation, delay the time of their inclusion. For the imperfect and sinful, purgatory is not God's wrathful, dreaded sentence on their sinfulness. It is his extended purifying hand to bring them fully to his love, a blessing of unsurpassing worth.

● ⁄⁌⁍ ●

Such is our speculative scenario. It should be noted that the severe and graphic imagery so often used in earlier discussions and descriptions of purgatory (which will be described in more detail in the Appendix) comes from a time, mindset, and cultural manner of thinking quite different from our own. Earlier Christians expressed their beliefs and religious convictions in more mythical, symbolic and metaphorical ways than we do. Though their descriptions of the afterlife sound highly realistic and "on-the-spot," much of what they were saying was not intended to be an actual eye-witness rendering of post-death realities. Rather it was an imaginative description of what they believed these realities to be and what was to be done about them. Ideas and beliefs for earlier Christians became all the more real the more concretely realistic they could imagine and express them. We might prefer a calmer, more abstract, logical and analytical explanation for our beliefs. They preferred to express their beliefs in concrete and arresting visual images as did their ancestors before them.

So the task of modern believers should be not to dismiss earlier theologies and descriptions of purgatory as naive, medieval and therefore superstitious and untrue. No, the Church teaches that behind all these imaginative descriptions lie very important religious truths. The task of contemporary believers should be to penetrate beneath the heightened imagery to discover the underlying meaning and repercussions of these truths.

The descriptions are more metaphorical than literal; they capture aspects of the message God has given us to make sense of our lives. They inform us how we should properly live them. Our task is to translate traditional beliefs into terms and images that will be more meaningful to our present mindset, not to dismiss them as naive and therefore irrelevant.

Chapter 7

Praying for the Dead

It is a holy and wholesome thought to pray for the dead (2 Mac 12:46).

Most of us have great love for our family and friends and mourn them deeply when they die. In death they remain vividly in our thoughts and memories. Spiritually one with them before they died, we know that we continue in that union after death.

Knowing how sinful and imperfect our own lives can be, how lacking in serious preparation for eternity we sometimes are, we can assume that others could die not fully prepared for the glory God intends for them. Our love for the dead should move us to assist them as they face judgment and ready themselves for heaven.

Prayer is the best way we can help the dead and manifest

our love for them. Prayerfully we should ask God to grant them the grace and strength they need to bring them fully into his love. And in our prayers we can also pledge to perform acts of kindness and charity toward others as a way of showing God our pleas for our loved ones are truly sincere.

There are many ways to express ourselves in prayer. We can pray for our dead in formal ways through prayers found in prayer books. Some examples will be given here. We can express our prayers spontaneously from the deeply felt emotions and desires of our heart. We can prayerfully contemplate the goodness of God and his will to save and fulfill all of his creatures, including in that contemplation our desire that our dead be soon fully in his love. The important thing is not how we pray, but that we pray for our dead in ways that we find comfortable. As body-spirit people, it is natural for us to give some kind of prayerful formulation and outward expression to the inner sentiments of our hearts. We should express what we feel in a tangible way. That, after all, is how we are made. We are spirits who express ourselves in an external bodily way.

We know that God wants us to help and pray for each other. He has given us Jesus as our premier model. He prayed to the Father often for his needs; he urged people to pray for others as they faced their various trials and crises. Jesus assured us that the Father listens attentively to all our prayers. The history of Christianity from Christ to our time is replete with evidence that prayer and selfless works done for the dead are helpful and efficacious. Can any of us doubt that the prayerful life and works of Mother Theresa had a good effect on the spiritual needs of the dying and dead she labored among? How could God not be moved by the good life and prayers of such a person?

From a very early period, Christians have also devoutly prayed for their dead by remembering them at Mass. We knew that the saving act of Jesus was present in this Supper. In his death we find the forgiveness of our sins. In his Resurrection he makes available to us the life and love of God. In the Mass, Jesus encases his saving act in a form that makes it possible for us to unite with it. What the dead need more than all else is full participation in the graces of Jesus' dying and rising. Our celebration of the Mass for their spiritual needs petitions these graces for them. Surely it is the highest form of help we can offer them.

In this action-event, the human Jesus made his ascent to God. How better to pray that our dead successfully make their final ascent than by joining them and ourselves in spirit to Christ's saving act? We should never think it strange or unusual to unite ourselves and the needs of those we love to Jesus' Eucharistic prayer. Indeed, he wants us to: "Do this in my memory — proclaim my death and Resurrection always — unite with it — what I've done here is *for you*."

We believe that the most saintly in death will quickly be assimilated into God's eternal love. The rest of us, because of our inadequacies and imperfections, quite likely will die with some purification work still to be done.

Jesus will surely be there to help us complete this work and he will be "most" with us as our living friends and the saints in heaven join with us in the mutual celebration of his saving death and Resurrection. We remember our dead at Mass not to barter their admission to heaven, but to petition Christ's paschal graces for them as they undertake their final purgatory preparation. Should they enter heaven sooner than we know, our union with Christ and his death and Resurrection at Mass becomes a perfect thanksgiving for their arrival there.

Some Prayers for the Dead

Eternal rest grant unto them, O Lord, and let perpetual light shine upon them. May the souls of the faithful departed, through the mercy of God, rest in peace. Amen.

Lord, my friend has died. Losing his/her presence and company saddens me greatly. I pray that he/she will soon be clothed with your light an eternal peace. To that end, I pledge my earnest prayers and acts of kindness toward others to hasten the day when you will draw my friend fully into the embrace of your love. May I live in a way that will cause you to draw me fully into your gracious love as well. I yearn to live eternally with you and there find again the company of my friend and loved ones.

I pray for, N. May all the saints support him/her with their prayers and intercessions. May they help ready the soul of my friend to meet and be with God. May Christ grant his eternal peace and may his light shine on this soul always.

Lord, I pray that you forgive the sins and imperfections of the dead. Purify and cleanse their love for you, so that they may live with you in peace and happiness forever. I pledge my prayers for their spiritual needs.

Heavenly Father, we mourn the death of our loved ones. Cleanse them and help their love for you to grow ever more perfect, so that they may live with you in joy forever. We ask this through Christ our Lord.

Lord, I pray for my departed friend whose salvation means so much to me. May his/her soul be cleansed of all that could defer his/her full coming to you. I promise my continued prayers and pledge good works to assist my friend in acquiring the joys you have prepared for all those who believe in you.

Comfort, Lord, the souls of the dead. Cleanse their hearts that your light may shine fully within them. May they soon experience your loving presence.

Remember, Lord, your servants who have departed this

world with the sign of faith. May their faith and strong love for you grant them a place of comfort, light and peace in your kingdom.

Lord, pour forth your graces and mercy on the dead. May they not long be delayed from entering fully into your love. May their temporary sufferings purify them and lead them quickly into your presence, so that they may praise your glory forever.

O God, life of the living, life of the dead. I know your love for me is eternal, and so it is for them. Let me never forget my loved ones who have died. May my faithfulness to them through prayers and selfless works be a sign to you of my firm belief in you, of my eternal love for you and them.

O God, we pray that the dead experience your presence and love face to face. May they love you with the intensity with which you love them. In their eternal happiness, may they remember our spiritual needs as we at death remembered them.

Mary, pray with me for my loved ones who have died. I loved them on earth. I love them in death. I ask that you pray with me for their eternal happiness. You knew the pains of suffering and loss. Strengthen me in my loss and intercede for my loved ones. My hope and theirs is in the Resurrection. My trust and theirs is in your Son. May he grant them eternal peace and everlasting happiness.

The Feast of All Souls

This annual Mass for all the faithful departed was first introduced into the liturgical calendar by the monastery of Cluny in France in the eleventh century. It spread through the Cluniac monasteries, and in short time was adopted and celebrated by most of the countries of Europe, and in time by their colonies around the world. Its date is November 2 (November 3 when the second falls on a Sunday). Celebrated so closely to the feast of All Saints (November 1), All Souls seems in some ways designed to be a theological balance to that feast. It reminds us that death does not mean automatic "sainthood" in heaven for all believers. Some souls obviously die needing further purification. The Feast of All Souls reminds the living to give spiritual assistance to the dead through prayers and good works.

Appendix

The Graphic Imagery of Purgatory

As Christians began to believe in a process of further purification for some of their dead, they used exceedingly graphic and severe imagery to describe it. Where today we might prefer a calmer, more reasoned, and reflective analysis of purgatory's purpose and necessity, earlier Christians chose to picture it with a harshness and severity that makes modern believers uncomfortable — blazing pits of fire, torments of every imaginable kind, etc. Where few Christians could legitimately claim to have seen the realities of life beyond the grave, we might wonder where all these supposed eyewitness accounts and descriptions of purgatory came from. What meaning did earlier believers intend by using this graphic imagery?

Since belief in purgatory as a distinct intermediate station of post-death existence took time to evolve and gain its separate identity, much of its earliest descriptive imagery seems to derive from scriptural images of hell. In fact, Augustine and other early fathers (as well as some Jewish rabbis of the first and second centuries A.D.) divided hell (*gehenna*) into two parts: a lower hell, a place of eternal punishment, and an upper hell, a place of temporary purgational suffering after which souls were able to leave and reach heaven. Just as hell was described as a pit or furnace of blazing unquenchable fire, a place of torment, moaning, weeping, gnashing of teeth, where worms die not, etc., so the purgational process was seen in like terms. The big difference, of course, was that its pains and sufferings were seen to be temporary and preparative for ultimate arrival in heaven. Further depictions of purgatory, like those given for hell, seem to be imagined opposites to the biblical joys of heaven (a place of rewards, blessings, treasures, where believers have fuller knowledge and wisdom and dwell in face-to-face vision of God, etc.).

The Imagery of Other Peoples

Moreover, as Jews were often influenced by the religions and religious terminology of neighboring peoples, borrowing and modifying the ideas of others to conform to their own beliefs, so Christians in time will borrow and use afterlife imagery from these same people. Egypt, for example, had a hell, and gave it a forbidding detail that reminds us of later descriptions of purgatory. Like the Egyptians, Christians will have their blazing pits as well as their lakes and rivers of fire where the wicked are subjected to violent torments. The beasts and demons that sometimes inhabit purgatory can also be found in Egyptian descriptions of hell. So Egypt could well be a contributor to the "imagery deposit" from which Christians will draw as they attempt to describe purgatory.

Persian Zoroastrianism also seems to have contributed to

the "imagery deposit" available to Christians as they described the afterlife. In Persian belief, the dead, both good and bad, are tested as they await judgment. The frequently used Christian image of purgatory as a narrow and dangerous bridge from earth to heaven is found in Persian religious literature as well. Purgatory's depiction as a place of darkness corresponds to Babylonian pictures of the other-world in the *Gilgamesh* epic. In Babylonian thought, the dead who were loved and cared for by the living seem to fare better than those who were unloved and unremembered — an aspect that is also found in Christian teaching about purgatory.

Hinduism had little influence on Christian imagery of purgatory in earlier centuries, but its influence grew in the Middle Ages and beyond as its religious ideas became more known to Christians. Hindu images served to reinforce Christian pictures of purgatory. Fire, a key Christian image, appears frequently in the burial rituals and theology of the Hindu dead. Three classes of the dead emerge from Hindu fire. The very good move on to an eternal spiritual realm. The grossly evil are returned by reincarnation to earth to be punished and ultimately seem headed for hell. The part-good, part-bad are reincarnated to try again to live better lives. Christians obviously reject reincarnation, but the categories of the Hindu dead seem to have some slight affinity to the post-death divisions of souls in Christian belief.

It is not inconceivable that Greece and Rome could have provided Christians usable imagery for some of their descriptions of purgatory. The classical writers gave vivid pictures of the underworld to which all the dead descended. There they were judged by the gods and suffered punishments proportionate to their violations of justice during their lifetimes.

Some of the most striking images we have of life beyond death are found in Virgil's *Aeneid*, where the hero visits the underworld and describes it in great detail. Many scholars believe that Virgil was the poetic model for Dante's *Divina*

Commedia; in fact, Virgil himself serves the role of guide for Dante's trip through the world beyond death. In his descriptions of this world, Dante uses images very similar to those used by Virgil. Other medieval commentators were also familiar with Virgil and borrowed or adapted his imagery of the next world. As Christians see heaven in the distance beyond purgatory, so Virgil has his Elysian Fields as an alternative paradise of repose for the just. He blames much of the pain and suffering of the underworld on people's ingrained sinfulness. Many of the punishments he narrates seem designed to cleanse and "burn out" of people the stains of sin — a familiar theme in medieval explanations of purgatory.

Plutarch, the Greek biographer and moralist, recounts dramatic tales of people whose souls took flight to the next world and saw there the fate of the dead, both the good and the bad. The images used to illustrate the lot of the bad are severe and violent. The descriptions of the just are pleasant and attractive. The souls in purgatory will bear many likenesses to Plutarch's descriptions of the world of the dead.

Christian writers seem to have borrowed freely from all these sources for their ideas of expiation and purification.

Judaism

Does traditional Judaism with its belief in *Sheol* as the home of the dead provide imagery serviceable to Christians as they seek to explain purgatory to themselves and others? It seems the static quiet and lack of punishment or purificational activity in *Sheol* offer no graphic pictures Christians can adopt and use. But in intertestamental Judaism, the divisions of the dead are more sharply drawn. In the rabbinical writings of the first and second centuries of the Christian era, the wicked are separated from the just and punished in *gehenna*. Some rabbis of that time proposed a geography of the next world with more detail than Jews had ever given it before. This literature saw souls at death going to one of three places.

The very wicked went to *gehenna* permanently. The less evil, partially good went to *Sheol* as a temporary waiting or intermediate state. The Jewish hell thus seems to have two parts to it. The souls of the just went to eternal reward in Eden, seen as a seventh heaven. So in many ways some Jews at this early period of Christian history seem to be moving in the direction Christians later moved as they become more certain of their belief in an intermediate state for some of the dead.

Jewish Apocalyptic

Many scholars today find much of purgatory's vivid imagery traceable to the apocalyptic literature of both Jews and Christians, especially that which was produced around the time of Christ and the early centuries of the Christian era, when apocalyptic preaching and writing flourished. For the most part, conservative Jews rejected this Judaeo-Christian apocalyptic literature. They thought it contained inauthentic teaching and labeled it "apocrypha." In time, Christians also rejected most of these writings. An important exception is the *Apocalypse of John*, the Book of Revelation, which was accepted by Christians, but not without controversy. Through the centuries, much of this literature was preserved and translated into Latin and the vernacular languages. In the late Middle Ages, its next-world imagery became popular with Christians, just when purgatory was reaching the climax of its doctrinal evolution.

What medieval Christians seemed to find most interesting about this literature were the many journeys to the hereafter that the apocalyptic seers were described as making.

A famous example of these excursions to the afterlife in Jewish apocalyptic is the journey of Enoch. An angel transports him to a place where some souls blaze like fire. He sees the waters of life but also rivers of fire. Other places are in utter darkness. Enoch is led to an abyss, the pit of hell, where pillars of fire shoot upward. He asks where souls reside before judgment and discovers that they dwell in different remote regions of the earth. He is shown a mountain that has four cavities, three shrouded in darkness, one filled with light that possesses a refreshing spring. He is told this is where souls await judgment. The various cavities are where souls are separated into different areas, depending on their guilt or innocence and the extent of suffering they experienced during their lives. The cavity of light appears to be the waiting place for martyrs and the saintly, for whom little punishment is in store. Those dwelling in the darker cavities can expect to suffer certain punishments after judgment. Eternal punishment will be the lot of the severely wicked.

Enoch's vision-journey contains several elements that later will be found in medieval depictions of purgatory. We see hell as a pit from which there is no escape. There is a mountain where souls await judgment. For some Jews there is an intermediate state of punishment between death and judgment. Also souls are punished proportionately, depending on the seriousness of their sins.

Another Jewish apocalyptic work, the fourth book of Ezra, was quoted by a number of early Church fathers. This work says that those who sin seriously and break the law are deserving of an eternal punishment in sadness and tears. Ezra has souls in the afterlife divided into seven different ranks or categories. Heaven is in the distance, and the souls of those who observed the law and lived basically good lives seem to be moving in that direction. It seems one can find here elements of the Christian idea of purgatory in the several ranks of the dead. Moreover, the post-death status of many seems to be a purifying preparation for heaven. It should be noted the Book of Ezra was very popular with Christians in the late Middle Ages.

Christian Apocalyptic

Christianity in its earliest centuries also had its apocalyptic "seers" who claimed visions of the afterlife. Three non-canonical apocalyptic books seem to have had an influence on the imagery of purgatory — the apocalypses of Peter, Ezra, and Paul.

The *Apocalypse of Peter* was written in Alexandria in Egypt around the end of the first century or early into the second century. For a time it was accepted in the canon of Scripture, but was finally excluded in 397. The book contained very elaborate descriptions of hell and the punishments it considered suitable for sinners to suffer there. Some of hell's imagery was transferred to purgatory. These included fire, flames, smoke, and lakes of blood in an atmosphere of forbidding darkness amid the loud cries and pleas of the dead. Those who lived good lives have access to Christ and his grace and dwell in pleasant surroundings. The punishments of sinners are severe and seen as deserved because sin violates God's justice.

The Christian *Apocalypse of Ezra*, which also was popular in the Middle Ages, seems to have supplied Christians with some images for purgatory. Though most of the seer's descriptions of the suffering of sinners were intended originally only for the damned, Christians in time transferred these to the sufferings of purgatory. In Ezra we find the images of fire, boiling lakes, the bridge, the many punishments. Fire-breathing animals are pictured guarding the places of torment. Though sinners suffer much, the just remain unaffected and do not suffer. Villains of history, such as Herod and other princes and rulers, are seen suffering for the evils they encouraged and perpetrated. Dante seems to have had knowledge of Ezra and included in his vision of the afterlife historical acquaintances who suffer for their villainies and sins. Ezra pictures steps going down and up. Dante will also have his stairs — the downward (to hell), the upward (to heaven).

The *Apocalypse of Paul*, a work composed in Egypt in the third century, seems to have had the greatest influence on medieval works about purgatory. Many copies and translations of this work were available to medieval commentators. The writer-seer writes as though he were detailing what Paul saw in his ecstatic transportation to the heavens (2 Cor 12:1-7). Most of the common purgatorial images are here also — the flaming trees, wheels, the rivers and ovens of fire; a great variety of punishments; the two sections of hell, one eternal, one temporary from which merciful liberation and transportation to paradise was possible; the animals, dragons and serpents guarding the places of punishment; regions of extreme cold where naked sinners suffer; the bridge over stormy waters; the overall darkness; the copious tears and pleas of the suffering — a veritable *Roget's Thesaurus* of images for medieval writers to borrow from as they attempt to describe the purgatory they have come to believe in. Again, this apocalypse sees the suffering of the sinful as necessary to satisfy divine justice.

Vision-Journeys of the Middle Ages

Quite likely influenced by the general dramatic structuring that ancient pagan religions gave to the next world, and having some knowledge of the picturesque images that Jewish and Christian apocalyptic seers gave to the fate of souls beyond death, the Middle Ages produced many examples of its own of imaginary vision-voyages to the next world. These too will help to solidify the images that believers at the time find suitable to describe the lot of sinners in purgatory. As the apocalyptic writings of an earlier time could be classified as a special religious literary genre for revealing messages from God about his will for the world and the purpose and destiny of life, so the many medieval accounts of visions of the next world seem to be later forms of the same genre.

To modern believers the dramatic imagery of these visions seems excessive, grossly unreal, and cruel. But we should realize that people of an age earlier than our own thought about and expressed their beliefs differently from the way we think and express ourselves today. We tend to line up our thoughts and ideas more methodically and logically, analyzing them more philosophically and reflectively. Earlier peoples often saw spiritual truth in more mythical and symbolic ways. To them the mythical was not unreal or untrue. It was a natural way of expressing transcendental truths and spiritual realities that were important to them — truths, for example, about the meaning, purpose, and destiny of human life. To them myths and symbolic pictures could very simply be seen as the encasement of spiritual truths in dramatic stories and images. So, many of the descriptions we find in earlier literature about heaven, hell and purgatory are not literal eyewitness descriptions of these "places." Rather, they are memorable and dramatic images that encase "truths" about these places in mythical and symbolic terms. Modern believers would be unwisely precipitous to reject the idea of purgatory because they consider earlier images of it exaggerated and excessive. They should make the effort to unwrap the mythical and biblical symbolism of the outer garments of purgatory and seek to arrive at its inner meaning and purpose.

In any event, the many vision-accounts of the next life that were composed in medieval times preserve much of the lush imagery of the earlier apocalyptic seers, giving it their own artistic variations and flourishes. Coincidentally, the native folklore of Celts, Germans, Scandinavians, and other converted European peoples often contained imagery similar to that used by Christians in their descriptions of life after death. This doubtless encouraged missionaries to continue to use such imagery as they explained Christian beliefs to these converted peoples. The earlier descriptive images of the fate of souls in the afterlife continue to appear in these vision-accounts. The main difference is that purgatory increasingly emerges with its own separate location and identity. These accounts gained great popularity with the literate faithful. They ultimately found their noblest and most fascinating expression in the magnificent work of Dante, the *Divina Commedia*.

The traditional images are all here: fire in every imaginable form (even volcanoes), working its purgative effects on souls in various ways; pools, lakes and rivers aflame and in turmoil, either cleansing or punishing souls according to their needs or deserts. Hell and purgatory are described as pits. In some visions, purgatory slowly evolves into the image of a mountain. The path from the grave to paradise is depicted frequently as a narrow and dangerous bridge which the just pass over with ease, while the unjust have all sorts of difficulties, often slipping into the dangerous and fiery waters below. The punishments sinners suffer appear to increase in number and seem aimed at the atonement of specific kinds of sins.

The "visionaries" who "witness" all the specifics of purgatory are often implored by suffering souls for their prayers to alleviate their pains and sorrows. Often souls gain some relief as the visionaries respond to their cries with promises of prayers and the doing of good works. This, of course, indicates that Christians in the Middle Ages believed that the prayers and works of the living could assist the spiritual needs of the dead. Almost invariably, the visionaries catch sight of paradise in these accounts (usually not too far from purgatory) and surround it with pleasing and attractive images — light, refreshing springs, cool breezes, greenery, flowers, pleasing fragrances — indicating that much of the sufferings in purgatory culminate in the acquisition of glory in the end.

We sense that these visions are designed to inform readers of the seriousness of life and the fate that awaits those who fail to take it seriously by living the virtuous lives the gospel asks them to live. Many of the visionaries who "witness" the graphic "realities" of the afterlife are sinners to begin with, who abandon their sinful ways for a life of virtue after their experience. Thus these accounts are also meant to motivate people to change the sinful direction of their lives. In other words, the writers obviously want to "scare the daylights" out of sinners. The accounts teach the theology of purgatory in very dramatic form. No one should underestimate their value in advancing and solidifying Christian belief in a post-death place of atonement and purgation for sinners.

Meaning of Purgatory's Imagery

Some of the imagery for purgatory appears time and time again. It is risky business to claim full knowledge of the exact meanings and connotations of the language used by people far removed from our time, culture and mindset. But perhaps it might be of some value to attempt a few educated surmises into why an earlier age considered certain images suitable to describe the goings on of purgatory. And we might note that our speculation into the meaning and appropriateness of their imagery will not be completely without reasonable basis, for the vision-accounts we've referred to occasionally specify the meaning of the imagery they use. Periodically the visionaries in these accounts fail to see the meaning of what they are witnessing. They ask their guiding angel to explain to them the meaning of things, and the angel in turn informs them why certain things must happen.

So first, we note the popularity of *fire*. It is the most common image associated with purgatory. Fire in every conceivable form seems to assail and overwhelm sinful souls. Modern believers, perhaps thinking in too univocal and literal a way, are naturally repulsed by the idea that God would punish sinners with real fire. What they fail to realize is that the descriptions of the suffering of these souls are not meant necessarily to be literal portrayals of the manner of their suffering. More likely they are symbolic and metaphorical images of the purification sinful souls are in need of in order to overcome the debilitating effects of their sins; figuratively they show God is preparing these souls for glory.

Fire is a biblical metaphor for God (Ps 50:3). Sins that are not fully requited at death must be submitted to his "atoning fire." This fire was also seen by earlier Christians to be a purifying instrument. Souls sullied by sins and selfishness need this purification before they can rightly enter God's presence. Fire, then, was seen to be a symbol of the divine punishment sins deserve. Figuratively it also represented God's efforts to purify and prepare souls for heaven. In a sense the fires of purgatory were like Christ's foretold baptism of fire (Mt 3:11; Lk 3:16). They repair and complete the Christian's baptism of water which sin has stained and compromised. As literal fire destroys the evil in things, so "God's fire" destroys the moral evil that remains in the soul at death. It cleanses and purifies souls of all the elements of evil that can impair their capacity for glory. Finally, for Jews and earlier Christians fire was seen as a symbolic image for God's judgment. For Christians at least, purgatory is a consequence of the judgment of God on the lives of the dead.

Another dominant image that occurs in descriptions of purgatory is water, great quantities of it in all its forms — seas, lakes, rivers, pools. Often these waters are stormy and dangerous; sometimes they are ablaze with fire where souls struggle and flounder about. Like fire, the waters seem also to be instruments of divine punishment for unrequited sins. And, of course, water was also regarded as a means of divine cleansing. That so many souls survive their watery sufferings shows that they are not being abandoned by God. As they atone for their sins, they are also being purified and prepared for their ultimate arrival in heaven. These waters, then, are symbolic of purgatory's purpose and function. It is a place of atonement and purification.

An image of purgatory that frequently appears in the literature is that of the narrow bridge, one end of which seems to be where souls at death begin their attempted crossing; the other, the terminal one, where heaven can be reached. Allowing for other more sophisticated and subtler meanings for the image, its main point seems to be that human life leads somewhere; it does not end with death or the grave. If departed souls come to it prepared, the bridge leads to heaven. Just souls have little difficulty traversing it, where others find the trip more than they can manage and fall precipitously into the darkness below. Since the bridge often spans the dangerous waters spoken about above, the implication seems to be that souls who sinned frequently must struggle to "the other side" by enduring the "watery sufferings" of divine punishment and purification symbolized by the dangerous (often fiery, demon-infested) waters below the bridge. Those who disappear beneath the waters entirely would seem to be the damned. Those who remain afloat and ultimately reach safe land after a great struggle seem to be the souls in purgatory.

The frequent image of purgatory as a pit (usually fiery, a place of many torments) was later transformed into a mountain. Jews and early Christians viewed the habitat of the dead to be below the earth, and this is probably why Christians first saw purgatory as a pit. Also a pit is a place of confinement with an opening at the top. This would indicate souls who go there for post-death reparative work will be able to find escape from the "place," once this work is done. Thus purgatory has its entrance, but also its exit. As purgatory was seen more and more to be an atoning and purifying preparation for heaven, the image of a mountain reaching from earth upwards toward heaven seemed to be a more suitable symbol. The struggle and trials unprepared souls suffered in their upward climb of the mountain seemed to show that their sufferings were not sheer punishment for their sinful deeds. They led and brought the "strugglers" ultimately to the heights of heaven.

The elaborate and ever more numerous specific torments and sufferings that afflict the souls of the sinful are quite likely dramatic images to indicate the extensive damage sin works on the soul. Sins not only generally do spiritual harm; they inflict damage on the soul in countless ways. The multitude of punishments tells sinners that all their various and sundry sins are not harmless peccadilloes undeserving of reparation, but are rather offenses that do serious harm. Since the various vision-accounts of life after death are read and heard by the living, the chronicling of these many punishments seems intended to warn the living to avoid free and easy attitudes toward sin. They should be serious about it, lest they be delayed at death and suffer like torments themselves.

So, the accounts warn and exhort the living to change their sinful ways and to live more virtuous lives. The loud cries and pleas of the dead for the living to pray and perform acts of charity on their behalf are obvious reminders to the living that they can indeed shorten the sad plight of the dead with their fervent prayers and good works. The fearsome animals, monsters and demons that dwell in various regions of the afterlife seem symbolic warnings of the difficulties all sinners will face if they fail to repent, seek forgiveness, and do penance for their sins.

Epilogue

A recent news item from the Associated Press about two people who obviously believed in purgatory:

Hamburg, Germany — The Hamburg-based *Bild* newspaper recently reported that a Spanish businessman and devout Roman Catholic stopped to pray at a church during a trip to Stockholm. As things turned out the visit made him a millionaire.

The church was empty except for a coffin containing the remains of a man, so Eduardo Sierra knelt down and prayed for the deceased for twenty minutes.

Sierra, 35, signed a condolence book after he saw a note saying all who prayed for the dead man should enter their names and addresses. He noticed he was the first to sign. He would be the only one.

Several weeks later he received a call from the Swedish capital informing him he was a millionaire.

Jens Svenson, the man he had prayed for, was a 73-year-old real-estate dealer who had no close relatives. He had specified in his will that "whoever prays for my soul is to receive all my possessions."

Glossary

Apocalypse, apocalyptic

From the Greek for uncovering, revealing. The writings and speech of Jewish and Christian seers (ca. 200 B.C. to A.D. 150) who claim divine knowledge concerning the culmination of world history (the end-time). They speak and write of this "event" and other things such as life beyond death with dramatic urgency, describing it with graphic pictures and symbolic images.

Apocrypha

From the Greek — hidden, obscure, not genuine. Jews label "apocrypha" and hold in suspicion those revelations not originally written in Hebrew. More generally, these are books that are doubtfully written by their claimed authors and whose revelations are considered questionable.

Canon, canonical

From the Greek — principle, norm, rule. The term relates to the books believers accept as authentic Sacred Scripture.

Eschatology

From the Greek *eschaton* — the end, the final reality. Eschatology is the theology that speaks about the last things, the end of the world, and judgment.

Exegesis, exegetical

From the Greek — an explanation, interpretation. The endeavor to determine what authors of an earlier time period intended their words to say to their original readers.

Expiation, atonement, reparation

Used here interchangeably to indicate the acts that seek to

make amends for sins and crimes and to repair their harmful effects.

Gehenna

From the Latin, derived from the Hebrew *ge-hinnom*. In the Old Testament, the valley of Hinnom near Jerusalem, where refuse was dumped and continuously burned to prevent pestilence. It became an image for hell as a place for the punishment of the wicked.

Glory

Used here to denote the mystery whereby God reaches out and communicates his presence, power and love to his creation.

Kenosis

From the Greek — an emptying (self-emptying). The key textual use of the term is in Philippians 2:6-11, which refers to the human Jesus' life and death as one of service to others. Possessing great powers and gifts, Jesus constantly gives (or empties himself) of these in service of others. As a result, at death through his Resurrection his humanity receives the fullness of exaltation and glory.

Myth, mythical

From the Greek *mythos* — word, story, legend. Used here for stories, dramatic and picturesque images and symbols, personifications, metaphors, etc., that seek to make the ultimate realities about human life, its meaning, purpose, destiny, and its hopes and problems, vivid, realistically concrete, and immediate.

Sheol

In the Old Testament, an unpleasant place of dark stillness in the depths of the earth, where the dead are thought to dwell; the underworld.

Select Bibliography

Ancient Christian Writers, Nos. 13, 19, 28, 30, 43, 44, 46, 47, 48 (Westminster, MD-NY: Newman/Paulist Press, 1951-1988).

Arendzen, J.P., *Purgatory and Heaven* (New York: Sheed & Ward, 1960).

Bartmann, B., *Purgatory* (London: Burns, Oates & Washbourne, Ltd., 1936).

Bastian, R.J., "Purgatory," *New Catholic Encyclopedia*, Vol. XI, pp. 1034-1039 (New York: McGraw-Hill Book Co., 1966).

Boros, L., *The Mystery of Death* (New York: Herder & Herder, 1965).

Brogan, B., "Eschatological Teaching of the Early Irish Church," *Biblical Studies, The Medieval Irish Contribution*, Ed., M. McNamara, pp. 46-58 (Dublin: Dominican Publications, 1976).

Catherine of Genoa (St.), *On Purgatory* (New York: Sheed & Ward, 1946).

Chicago Studies, Vol. 24, No. 2, August 1985, "Armageddon" (whole issue on Eschatology).

Dante, *The Comedy of Dante Alighieri*, Cant. II (*Il Purgatorio*) Trans., Dorothy L. Sayers (Baltimore: Penguin Books, 1955).

Select Bibliography

The Fathers of the Church, Vols. 39, 58 (Washington, DC: Catholic University of America Press, 1959, 1966).

Fortman, E.J., *Everlasting Life after Death* (New York: Alba House, 1976).

Fransen, P., "The Doctrine of Purgatory," *Eastern Churches Quarterly*, No. 13, 1959.

Gleason, R., *The World to Come* (New York: Sheed & Ward, 1959).

Guardini, R., *The Last Things* (New York: Pantheon, 1954).

Klinger, E., "Purgatory," *Sacramentum Mundi*, Vol. 5, pp. 166-168, Ed., K. Rahner (New York: Herder & Herder, 1970).

Küng, H., *Death and Eternal Life* (London: 1984).

Le Goff, J., *The Birth of Purgatory* (London: Scholar Press, 1984). By far the best current historical survey and commentary on the development of the doctrine of purgatory, to which the author of the present work is heavily indebted.

Maloney, G.A., *The Everlasting Now* (South Bend: Ave Maria Press, 1980).

O'Donnell, J.J., *Confessions* (Augustine's), Vols. I-III (Oxford: Clarendon Press, 1992).

Ombres, R., *Theology of Purgatory* (Dublin and Cork, 1978).

Phan, P.C., "Contemporary Context and Issues in Eschatology," *Theological Studies*, Vol. 55, No. 3, September 1994, pp. 507-556.

Rahner, K., *On the Theology of Death* (New York: Herder & Herder, 1961).

—, Theological Investigations, Vols. II, IV (Baltimore: Helicon Press, 1963, 1966).

—, Theological Investigations, Vol. XIX (New York: Crossroad, 1983).

Ratzinger, J., *Eschatology, Death and Eternal Life* (Washington, DC: Catholic University of America Press, 1988).

Taylor, M., Ed., *The Mystery of Suffering and Death* (New York: Alba House, 1973).

Troisfontaines, R., *I Do Not Die* (New York: Desclee Co., 1963).

van de Walle, A.R., *From Darkness to the Dawn* (Mystic, CT: Twenty-Third Publications, 1985).

Scriptural Index

Genesis

3:17-19   20

6-9   20

Numbers

20:12   20

2 Maccabees

12:39-46   21-22

12:45 (46)   19, 21, 83

2 Samuel

12:14   20

Psalms

50:3   99

Isaiah

52-53   44

53:4-5   20-21

Matthew

3:11   100

5:48   49, 53, 59

7:12   46

7:17   46

12:31-32   18, 23

16:27   49, 53, 59, 70

Mark

8:34-35   49, 53, 59, 62

10:43-44   45

Luke

3:16   100

11:28   61

23:43   63

John

5:28-29   59-60

5:29   24, 31, 49, 53

13:15   46

15:14, 16-17   46, 49, 53

Romans

3:25   63

5:5   47

8:31-39   58

9:14-18   62

13:8   46

1 Corinthians

3:10-15   23, 29, 33, 44

3:15   18

3:16-17   25

6:9   24, 49, 60

6:9-10   24, 49, 60

6:15   25

10:17   25

12:12-14   8

13   42-43, 46

2 Corinthians

5:10   49, 53, 60, 71

12:1-7   95

Philippians

2:6-11   50-51, 105

Colossians

1:24   52

2 Thessalonians

2:28   57

1 Timothy

2:3-6   14, 58, 65

2:6   44

2:5-6   21, 44

Hebrews

12:14   24

1 Peter   18, 24

Revelation

21:27   7, 25

Index of Names and Subjects

Adam 20, 57
Aeneid 91
All Souls Day 33, 87-88
apocalypse, apocalyptic 93-97, 104
apocrypha 93, 104
atonement 19, 21-22, 29, 32, 35, 53, 63, 98-100, 104
Babylonian beliefs 91
baptism 25, 28
  of fire 100
  of water 100
Bede 33
Body of Christ (Mystical) 26, 64
bridge (as purgatory image) 32, 91, 95, 96, 98, 100-101
canon, canonical 33, 95, 104
Catechism of the Catholic Church 4, 18
Church, Eastern 17, 30, 34-35
Church, Western 17, 30, 34-35
Clement of Alexandria 26, 28
Cluny (monastery) 33, 87
communion of saints 35
Confessions (of St. Augustine) 28-29
Cyprian 28
Dante 33, 36-37, 56, 91-92, 95, 97
David 20
death, new theology of 13-14, 15
Divina Commedia 33, 36-37, 97-99
Egypt, Egyptians 90, 95
Enoch 93-94
eschatology, eschatological 32, 57, 104, 106-108
exaltation 51-52, 105
exegesis, exegetical 25, 104
expiation 12, 15, 30-31, 35, 63, 92, 104
Ezra 94-95
final option 13, 14, 69-73

fire (as purgatory image) 18, 23-24, 28, 29, 32, 33, 44, 55-56, 64, 89-91, 93, 95-97, 99-100, 101
Florence, Council of 8, 17-18, 35
folklore 97
forgiveness 9, 19, 21, 23, 30-32, 35, 40, 45, 48, 71-72, 84, 102
freedom 13, 45, 70
funerals
  present liturgical emphasis 9-11
  sermons 10
gehenna (see hell) 90, 92-93, 105
geography of the afterlife 34, 92-93
Gilgamesh Epic 91
glory 9-12, 24, 28-29, 31, 33, 37, 41, 46-49, 51-52, 59, 61, 66-67, 69-70, 79, 83, 87, 98-100, 105
Greece 91
heaven (see paradise) 7-8, 10, 14, 18, 20, 24, 34, 36, 39-41, 43, 48, 50-53, 56, 60-61, 64-66, 71-73, 78-80, 83, 85, 88, 90-95, 97, 100-101, 106
hell (see *gehenna*) 8-9, 14, 33-34, 37, 48, 60, 90-91, 93-98, 105
Hindu, Hinduism 91
imitation (of Jesus) 50
indulgences 19, 35, 66
Irish 32, 106
Jesus Christ
  as model 50, 84, 72
  Resurrection of 9, 19, 47, 105
  Savior 50, 61, 72
Jews, Jewish, Judaism 8, 22, 26, 90, 93-94, 96, 100-101, 104
joy 10, 15, 37, 43, 47, 56, 86
Judas Maccabees 21
judgment 11-13, 15, 18, 32, 47, 49, 60, 71, 76-79, 83, 91, 93-94, 100, 104

kenosis (self emptying) 51-52, 64, 105

life, purpose of 14, 15, 41-42, 45-48, 60, 65, 69, 72, 96-97, 105

Lyons, Second Council of 8, 17, 19, 35

Mass(es) for the dead
  Requiem 9-10, 15
  of Resurrection 85
  why a suitable prayer 85-87

metaphor, metaphorical 24, 63, 80-81, 99

Middle Ages 32, 42, 55, 91, 93-96, 98

Mother Theresa 84

mountain 33, 36-37, 94, 98, 101

myth, mythical 80, 97, 105

Noah 20

Origen 26, 28

paradise (see heaven) 8, 10, 48, 52, 56-57, 63, 80, 92, 96, 98

Pelagianism 60-61

Persia 90-91

pit (as purgatory image) 33, 90, 93-94, 101

Plutarch 92

prayers for the dead, 83-87

purgatory
  core doctrine of 39-45
  doctrinal, traditional history of 17-38
  in New Testament 14, 23-26, 29, 42-43, 48-54, 57-60, 61, 62
  in Old Testament 20-21, 63
  legalistic, juristic understanding of 44
  new theology of 45-53, 69
  objections to 55-67
  rationale for 17-38
  seen as punishment 19, 33, 44, 55, 63-65, 90, 96, 97-99
  time and space imagery 32-33

reformers (Protestant) 35

reincarnation 91

reparation 12, 15, 40, 49, 101, 104

resurrection of Christians 19, 28

Rome 91

Sacrament of Penance and Reconciliation 12

salvation, essential meaning of 28, 33, 41, 60-61

selfishness 7, 20, 31, 36, 40, 51, 56, 65, 71-72, 79, 99

selflessness 14, 31, 40, 48, 64

Sheol 92-93, 105

sin, contemporary views of 12-13, 15
  consequences of 12-13, 20
  general understanding 12-13, 40
  need for punishment 12, 19, 20, 44, 52, 63-64, 79
  Old Testament stories about 63

spirituality 36, 38, 66

St. Augustine 28 30, 44, 75, 90

St. Catherine of Genoa 56

St. Gregory the Great 18, 31-32

St. Paul 25, 29, 42, 44, 47, 50, 52, 95-96

St. Perpetua 26-27

St. Peter 24, 95

symbol, symbolic 80, 97, 99-101, 102, 104

temple 25

Tertullian 26-28

torments (in purgatory) 32, 44, 63, 89-90, 101-102

Trent, Council of 8, 17-18, 35

Virgil 91-92

vision-stories 26-27

vision-journeys 96-99

water (as purgatory image) 27, 100

Yahweh 63

Zoroastrianism 90

Our Sunday Visitor...
Your Source for Discovering the Riches of the Catholic Faith

Our Sunday Visitor has an extensive line of materials for young children, teens, and adults. Our books, Bibles, booklets, CD-ROMs, audios, and videos are available in bookstores worldwide.

To receive a FREE full-line catalog or for more information, call **Our Sunday Visitor** at **1-800-348-2440**. Or write, **Our Sunday Visitor** / 200 Noll Plaza / Huntington, IN 46750.

Please send me: __ A catalog
Please send me materials on:
   __ Apologetics and catechetics   __ Reference works
   __ Prayer books   __ Heritage and the saints
   __ The family   __ The parish

Name_____
Address_____Apt._____
City_____State___Zip_____
Telephone (   )_____

A89BBABP

Please send a friend: __ A catalog
Please send a friend materials on:
   __ Apologetics and catechetics   __ Reference works
   __ Prayer books   __ Heritage and the saints
   __ The family   __ The parish

Name_____
Address_____Apt._____
City_____State___Zip_____
Telephone (   )_____

A89BBABP

Our Sunday Visitor
200 Noll Plaza
Huntington, IN 46750
1-800-348-2440
OSVSALES@AOL.COM

Your Source for Discovering the Riches of the Catholic Faith